Marco Simoncelli
THE TRIBUTE BOOK

© 2012 RCS Libri S.p.A., Milan

First published in Italian by RCS Libri S.p.A. in September 2012
This English-language edition first published in September 2013

A catalogue record for this book is available from the British
Library

ISBN 978 0 85733 402 2

Library of Congress control card no 2013941308

Published by Haynes Publishing,
Sparkford, Yeovil, Somerset BA22 7JJ, UK
Tel: 01963 442030 Fax: 01963 440001
Int. tel: +44 1963 442030 Int. fax: +44 1963 440001
E-mail: sales@haynes.co.uk
Website: www.haynes.co.uk

Haynes North America Inc.,
861 Lawrence Drive, Newbury Park, California 91320, USA

Art and cover director: Sergio Pappalettera/Studio Prodesign
Design and layout: Gaia Daverio, Daris Diego Del Ciello/
  Studio Prodesign
Editorial: Anna Aiello, Andrea Canzanella, Daria Figari, Chiara
  Giusti, Angela Lombardo, Marianna Loy
Technical co-ordinator: Sergio Daniotti

Printed and bound in the USA by Odcombe Press LP,
1299 Bridgestone Parkway, La Vergne, TN 37086

Front cover photograph by Andrew Northcott

Marco Simoncelli

THE TRIBUTE BOOK

ROSSELLA & PAOLO SIMONCELLI

Foreword by **Valentino Rossi**

Edited by **Paolo Beltramo**

Translated by Heather Watson

FOREWORD

By Valentino Rossi

To those who did not have the chance to meet
Marco and now would like to know more about him,
I strongly recommend this book.

Simply because Sic was like this, exactly as his
closest friends and familiars describe him in the
following pages. I was among the lucky guys
who met him and had the pleasure to spend time
with him.

The thing we managed to do best was having
fun: with friends, with the bikes, with the cars…
The nice thing about Sic was his character: he was
fun, a really good person, but his best quality was
definitely that he was honest and authentic.

He always said what he thought, maybe at the
wrong time, but he was always honest. He was
always fair with friends and always defended those
who deserved it.

That's why he was so special. Thanks to this book
you can get an idea of who Sic was.

Have a good reading!

Marco at his first MotoGP
race, Qatar 2010, with his
friend Valentino.
(Gold and Goose)

MY SIC

By Paolo Beltramo

It was Rossella and Paolo who wanted this book to be compiled and I am honoured that they decided to entrust me with the task. I tried to speak with as many people as possible, those who loved Marco, those who knew him, those who were lucky enough to share something great, fun and important with him. Not everybody of course; that would have been impossible.

This tale tells of Marco Simoncelli as if he were still here with us. And through photos, memories and film clips I think it is really possible to relive him for a while. This book is like a full stop, without the new paragraph, that takes you back to the beginning and has you reread everything like a story that continues. A full stop that isn't final, but that serves as a reference, there to remind you that Marco is still there somewhere, and that perhaps he's laughing, talking crap. Or maybe he's racing, fighting, overtaking. Who knows?

If Marco is here inside, then this book has to be cheerful, fun, abundant, deep. Not just a book of memories, even if they are just that, but a chance to show Sic as he really was, from a young boy, from a time before bikes, to relive the journey that led him to be the strong, warrior-like rider and splendid person that he became. To understand where his values, strength and serenity – the qualities that led so many to fall in love with him over time – came from. In compiling the memories, I have decided to leave the written words as close as possible to each individual's way of speaking: this means that ungrammatical phrases or dialectal nuances are left in on purpose, because when we recount a story orally it is more alive, more immediate, more sincere and entertaining than when we use a language that is perhaps more correct, yet cold.

I am among those who were lucky enough to know and befriend Marco Simoncelli. I see this as a privilege because even if he was only 24, Marco would never disappoint from a human perspective. He had a way of presenting himself that was both mature and infantile, that made him spontaneous, friendly, funny and cheerful. He was capable of 'little-big' gestures; he could impart important messages by doing small things. In essence, he would transfer that correct, serene, straightforward and simple way of interpreting life on to you. You would always be happy in his company, whether at dinner, out and about, at the races, at home. And he was maturing a lot and didn't live, like so many other successful sportsmen, in a world detached from reality. On the contrary he was always closer to the real world. The small things made you realise this, you became increasingly conscious of it. In 2011 he didn't like the pressure associated with participating in the Japanese Grand Prix at Motegi, less than 100km from the Fukushima nuclear plant, damaged in the earthquake and tsunami a few months earlier. He began to admire Muhammad Ali for having courageously refused to go and fight in Vietnam and for his tenacity: 'Shit, he sure had balls...'

It was for this reason that I brought him a Muhammad Ali T-shirt to Australia, with Ali's name on the front and the motto 'Fly like a butterfly, sting like a bee' on the back. He wore it every day during that last GP in Malaysia, whether going to breakfast or to dinner in the hotel. He in turn gave me a funny one that he had bought in Las Vegas. When I saw him in the foyer wearing the Ali shirt, I went up to my room, put his shirt on and when we saw each other we were as pleased as punch: each wearing the other's gift. I gave him another T-shirt at Indianapolis, in 2010 – a Jimi Hendrix one. A while later he came to see me in Milan and when he got out of the car he was wearing that shirt – it was precisely those 'little-big' gestures that made him so special.

He felt people's pain and showed this when he sent me a text about the Philippines; yes, it was all beautiful, the sea, the resort, the weather but 'Shit, so many people suffering... Everyone should come here to understand first-hand.' Basically he would have made that rare and difficult step to link his sporting life to his real life and soon – I am sure of it – he would have put himself forward and used his popularity for a noble cause, for something that went beyond racing, that counted more than racing.

Just as Valentino wrote in his famous tweet, Marco was as sweet in life as he was tough on track. He was always competitive; whatever he was doing he would always give it his all. He needed, wanted to win as soon as possible, whether he was playing cards, Risk, karting with friends, skiing... If he didn't win, he had to play again, another go, another attempt. Characteristics that weren't contradictory, on the contrary they represented his personality perfectly; Marco wasn't one of those who needed to redress destiny or overcome childhood traumas. No, he raced because it was what he loved to do and he was determined because the races were to be taken seriously. The grit, the will to try, to never give up, to give it your all, this was all inside him, as natural as his jokes.

You could see he was a lot purer than the media by the way he would react spontaneously to things he saw as wrong or to the bad things that happened to him: he would get mad, he'd be disappointed, he'd cry, he'd laugh but then he'd react and start to work towards his goals again. He was never prepared for surprises that would... always surprise him. There in Kuala Lumpur, before the cursed race, we had gone to the airport together (not a long trip as a tunnel connects it directly to the hotel so it's only a three-minute walk) to meet Kate who was arriving from the Philippines with her mother. We headed over there, chatting, and he admitted to me that some of the controversy of the previous months had affected him during certain races, but after the fourth-place finish in Japan (due to a penalty, else he'd have been second) and second place in Australia just a few days previously, he was feeling better, ready, strong, sure. We continued to chat and to wait. More than an hour passed and there was no sign of Kate. He called her once, twice, three times until we worked out that she was waiting at the taxi rank, yes, but outside another terminal. And maybe we were the stupid ones, for not having thought of it, for not having found out. But the great thing was watching Marco, how he didn't get mad, how he stayed calm.

Anyway a guy who, one night outside my parents' house, started to play ball in the street with two guys he'd never seen before, you can't expect anything other than simplicity and enjoyment. He was able to continuously increase his number of friends without ever taking away from those he already had; an amazing ability to pay attention and to show affection, an extraordinary thing.

His kindness was beautiful and ran deep. One evening he wanted us to go and eat in Monza, at his friend's house. He came right into the centre of Milan to pick me up and he took me back home at about two, three in the morning – being nice was no effort for him.

One year, about November time, he asked me where I would be on 14 January the following year because he wanted me to present his party in Coriano. I'm sure he knew that I'd be in Brazil at that time, as I was every year, but he asked me anyway. When I told him that I'd be away he said: 'So can I ask Guido Meda?' When I of course agreed he rang Guido to say: 'Oh, Guido, seeing as Paolo will be in Brazil would you like to come and present my party?' Not candid but pure.

I really miss that physical way he had of showing friendship. Marco would always hug you, even if you saw him several times during the same day. It's true, as Aldo Drudi mentions in his contribution, that hugging him was like hugging a tree. I do that from time to time and it's a very positive, invigorating sensation. He was like that, he had strong, beautiful energy. And every dedication that I have from him finishes with 'a hug'.

While writing his autobiography I was often at his house in Coriano. The first time, Marco had only had his BMW M3 for a day or two. It was 2009 and he was still suffering with his right wrist that he'd broken at the Cava before leaving for the start of the championship in Qatar, and so he was going to Imola for physiotherapy. Kate and I were with him but I felt that the M3 didn't exactly feel like a 420bhp V8 should. 'It doesn't seem like it has so much horsepower, it feels like the one you had before. Are you sure you've got the settings right?' And he replied: 'Yes, it's on sport...' But he was perplexed and started to scroll through the menu at speed until he found 'sport plus'. He selected that option and the M3 transformed from a fast car into a beast. 'Shit, you were right, now she's moving!' he said, eyes sparkling. While we were at it we kept looking at the menus until we found speed selection for the alarm. Normally you'd set the 'beep' at 50kph if you want to be warned when you're going too fast in the city, or at 130kph on the motorway. At a certain point I said: 'I think it's good now.' He'd set it at 320... And that's where it remained.

He was always part of a group, there were always friends around him, many of whom you will meet in this book. At the races too, Marco would never eat without waiting for his team, especially once he found the right one, even if it was 10.30 at night. He would always sit in the middle of the table, never at the head. He'd never ignore anyone, he'd put you at your ease – a characteristic that never changed as his popularity and sporting success increased, he was like that in 2007 and was the same in 2011.

The day he won the 250 championship in Sepang he got to parc fermé, that cage where they put the top three bikes and riders – he was exhausted, dehydrated. When I saw him I offered him my bottle, half full of water and mineral salts: 'But then what will you do?' was his reply – he was on the verge of collapse but was worried about me!

One time I had done a live link with him for *Studio Sport* and at the end, to close, I had asked him something like: 'And so tomorrow?' 'A lot of throttle and less jerking around!' was his answer. 'Pardon, sorry?' 'A lot of throttle and less jerking around!' he repeated, laughing and becoming a hero in the Mediaset studio in the process.

In 2011, during post-practice interviews, he told me a couple of times that he was struggling to find those extra two or three tenths that he needed. As a joke I bent down and pretended to pick something up from the ground and told him: 'Here they are!' He pretended to take them and tuck them inside his leathers. So then I decided to print out 60 tenths on pieces of paper and give them to him in a little box. He always carried it with him and, when he finished second in Australia as well as during the cursed race in Malaysia, he had a couple of those tickets in his suit...

But he wasn't superstitious; he had decided that it wouldn't be the placing of a toothbrush, placed here instead of there, that would change the way things went. He wasn't even bothered if someone wished him 'Auguri!' instead of the traditional pre-race 'In bocca al lupo!' It only mattered that that person said it positively, with sincerity.

When his first MotoGP podium finally arrived at Brno I went to interview him after he'd changed. He had a pair of glasses hanging from the button of his shirt and at one point I asked him if he could hold the microphone for a minute. He took it, looking at me with that amused expression that he'd get when he was thinking: 'Let's see what this fraudster's up to.' I hugged him because I wanted to lift him up – joking as we often did – to check whether a weight had been lifted, whether he felt lighter. In doing so I broke his glasses.

'Lord, Paolo, now you owe me a pair of glasses!'

'But don't they come from the sponsor?'

'Yes but what's that got to do with it, you still owe me,' he replied, laughing. So at Indianapolis I went to a crap gift shop (the one where I got the Hendrix shirt) and found a pair of sunglasses, pink on the inside, black but covered in pink hearts on the outside. On him they were horrific, funny, so effeminate, he laughed like mad. They are at his house, Martina wears them now... They look great on her.

Together we came up with some funny scenes like the 'teleport' but I want to tell you what we had prepared for the last race of 2011 in Valencia – we never got to do it. We were going to wear handkerchiefs on our faces like bandits, while remaining recognisable, him with the team uniform and sponsored scooter with number 58 and his name. And we were going to go into the smaller teams' hospitality units – with water pistols or bubble guns – and steal salami and some beers. Then we were going to run back to his motorhome and eat and drink, hidden under the table. The Irta and Dorna guys would have 'arrested' us. And while they took us away with our hands behind our backs he would have said: 'But how did they catch us, we even had masks on!' Then I would have signed off, saying that our regular feature 'Tell me about Sic' would be back the following year. 'If they let us go in time...' would have been the closing joke. It remained an idea, a desire, a regret, a small unaccomplished dream, a bittersweet smile. Almost nothing, in the immense emptiness that I was left with once Marco was gone.

Marco Simoncelli's story, Sic's story, cannot continue. But what we can do is make sure that the story remains, that his life doesn't disappear, that the person lives on – in us, in our memories, in our hearts. This is the aim of the book: to tell the story of Marco, of Sic, so that he lives on forever.

PAOLO AND ROSSELLA SIMONCELLI, THE PARENTS.

MAURIZIO PASINI, FOUNDER OF THE PASINI MINI-PROJECT, LUCA'S BROTHER.

LUCA PASINI, FOUNDER OF THE PASINI MINI-PROJECT, THE TEAM WITH WHICH MARCO RACED MINIBIKES. MATTIA PASINI'S FATHER.

SIMONE CORSI, THE KID TO BEAT IN MINIBIKE RACES, MARCO'S TEAM-MATE IN GILERA IN 2006.

ANDREA DOVIZIOSO, THE LIFELONG RIVAL.

KATE FRETTI, THE GIRLFRIEND.

CARLO CASABIANCA, THE TRAINER.

RICCARDO ROSSI, MARCO'S COUSIN, DANIELE'S BROTHER.

DANIELE ROSSI, MARCO'S COUSIN, RICCARDO'S BROTHER.

VALENTINO ROSSI, THE 'BIG BROTHER', ON AND OFF TRACK.

MASSIMO MATTEONI, CREW CHIEF FOR TEAM MATTEONI RACING WHERE MARCO DEBUTED IN THE 125 CHAMPIONSHIP.

SANZIO RAFFAELLI (AKA 'MALABROCCA'), THE TRUSTED MECHANIC.

NICOLA PASTORE, MARCO'S LITERATURE TEACHER AT SECONDARY SCHOOL.

MATTIA TOMBESI, CLOSE FRIEND, CLASSMATE THROUGHOUT PRIMARY AND SECONDARY SCHOOL.

MAURO SANCHINI (AKA 'SANCHIO'), RIDER, SUPERBIKE COMMENTATOR AND MARCO'S CLOSE FRIEND.

SPEAKING ABOUT SIC

(In order of appearance)

CHIARA AIROLDI, 'KIA', KATE'S FRIEND.

MICHELE MASINI, 'MICKY', MARCO'S FRIEND AND MECHANIC FOR TEAM GRESINI RACING.

DINO COPPOLA, MARCO'S FRIEND.

GIAN MARCO GIANNINI, 'GIANMA', MARCO'S FRIEND.

MATTIA PASINI, TEAM-MATE IN MINIBIKE RACING AND LIFELONG FRIEND.

LUCIANO FROM THE 'PINETA' WHERE MARCO AND HIS FRIENDS WOULD HANG OUT.

RAFFAELE DE ROSA, FRIEND AND RIDER.

GIOVANNI CUZARI, CEO OF MEDIA ACTION.

GUIDO D'AMORE, MARCO'S NAVIGATOR DURING RALLIES.

ALDO DRUDI, DESIGNER RESPONSIBLE FOR MARCO'S GRAPHICS.

MICHELE PIRRO, FRIEND AND RIDER HAVING MET IN TEAM GRESINI RACING'S GARAGE.

FAUSTO GRESINI, MANAGER AND FOUNDER OF TEAM GRESINI RACING.

CARLO MERLINI, COMMERCIAL AND MARKETING DIRECTOR OF SAN CARLO HONDA GRESINI.

ALIGI DEGANELLO, GREAT FRIEND. MARCO'S CREWCHIEF FROM 2007 IN 250 WITH GILERA AND IN MOTOGP WITH HONDA. ELVIO DEGANELLO'S FATHER.

ELVIO DEGANELLO, MARCO'S ELECTRONICS TECHNICIAN FROM 2004.

CARLO PERNAT, MARCO'S SPORTING CONSULTANT FROM 2007.

PAOLO CASTELLI, THE PHYSIOTHERAPIST.

OUR
SIC

"EVERYONE IS A FAN ROUND HERE, OUR PARENTS HAD ENORMOUS PASSION AND THEY PASSED IT ON TO US. IT'S GREAT HERE BECAUSE MAYBE SOMEONE WHO LIVES IN VAL D'AOSTA HAS THE PASSION BUT THERE AREN'T MANY TRACKS IN VAL D'AOSTA, WHILE DOWN HERE IN EMILIA-ROMAGNA THERE ARE LOADS OF TRACKS FOR GO-KARTING, MINIBIKING..."

1. BOY RACERS

THE FIRST TIME

PAOLO One day, on the road back from Offida, the town where Marco's grandparents come from, we spotted the minibike track in Cattolica and decided to stop and make a lap. We were all together, Rossella and grandparents Italo and Felicia too, and were all in agreement about stopping, all except grandma, always a pain.

The track was closed that day but the owner was there doing some work, Panino his name was. You still see him today, riding around on his Lambretta, he's one of the supporters of Mattia Pasini's fan club. I got out and said: 'Look, my boy's never been on a minibike, maybe we could let him try seeing as there's no-one here...' And he agreed. He took the boy, put him on the bike and at the start he held on to the seat because everyone swerves all over the place on their first try.

But Marco moved away as if it was a natural thing for him. He began to go round and round, he must have lapped for 20, 25 minutes. Then he stopped, Panino looked him in the eye and told him: 'You can come when there are other people too.' I remember that phrase well, it was wonderful: 'You can come when there are other people too.'

The relationship with your father is amazing, the understanding is reciprocal and you're really a beautiful picture together. Let's not mention your father's pride at seeing you so self-assured on the bike because, I don't know if I have already told you about this in your diary, but for Christmas you received a beautiful motocross bike. Yesterday we went to the minibike track and you tried riding – I must say that you're really good. Coming back from school your father often lets you drive the car too, and you surprise me. You are certainly talented.

From Rossella's diary, 2001

"MY DAD AND I HAVE A WONDERFUL RELATIONSHIP. HE IS THE ONLY ONE WHO HAS SEEN ALL OF MY RACES, FROM THE VERY FIRST MINIBIKE RACE UP UNTIL TODAY. WHEN WE'RE AT THE RACES WE BEHAVE AUTOMATICALLY, HE KNOWS WHAT I NEED AND WE DON'T EVEN NEED TO SPEAK, WE ALWAYS UNDERSTAND EACH OTHER STRAIGHT AWAY. HE IS A FATHER AND A FRIEND... SOMETIMES A BIT OF A PISSED-OFF FRIEND! "

For a couple of weeks now your father has been taking you to the minibike track. You really like it, your dad perhaps even more so.

From Rossella's diary, 1993

A COMPLETELY RED POLINI

PAOLO Once Marco tried riding the minibike we were at the track every Sunday and, when we could, some weekday evenings too. Ten minutes, 20,000 lire. The first time that was enough, the second time too, the third time we had to pay for two sessions, until we got up to 100,000 lire and at that point I said: 'Hang on, maybe it makes sense to buy one.' We began to look for a bike and it was at that time that we met Manuel Poggiali and his father, Claudio. Claudio Poggiali was selling Manuel's first minibike, I remember that we went to San Marino to buy it. We were in their garage, and while we were deciding on a price this shy young boy came past. I said hi and got him to talk a little: 'I'm Manuel, I race minibikes'. It must have been '94, so Manuel was already in the Italian championship. The bike was a red Polini, completely red: in the end I wrote a cheque for 1.25 million lire.

We could then go riding whenever we wanted, paying only for the use of the track. We would spend whole afternoons, whole evenings there. Everything went well at first but then Marco faced the problem of getting his knee on the ground: it seemed simple but getting his knee down through the corner was a huge accomplishment for Marco. We were at the Miramare track when he did it for the first time, he stopped and was so happy, and I remember it even now. He was so hyped-up: 'Dad, I dragged my knee on the ground!' It was fundamental for him, more important than going fast, and once he'd learned how to do it he wanted to do it along the straight too, leaning even when there was no need to. Amazing!

ON TRACK

PAOLO There was a minibike boom at that time, it was the start of summer and in the evenings a certain Mattia Pasini would show up at Miramare. Damn, when Mattia Pasini came along he would lap us with every two laps he made... He'd really be on it, he'd leave us for dust... Marco watched him, a little envious, but I always said to him: 'Marco, don't worry, we are taking it a step at a time, a step at a time, a step at a time...' But already by the end of that summer we were running rings around him! That was Marco's character, he saw Mattia going fast but he didn't say 'I'll never be able to do that', no, he said 'I'm coming after you!' That was his strength; his desire to make it was truly incredible.

That summer, every Wednesday evening, Panino would organise unofficial races at the Cattolica track. All the kids that had minibikes knew that Wednesday evening meant racing at Cattolica and they would all meet there. I remember Pellino, who later became Marco's rival in the European 125 championship, and there was Manna, Tiraferri, Pasini... These kids were already fast and would even travel from far away to come to the races, one even from Spoleto. The nice thing is that everyone started together, both riders and non-riders, but Panino had decided that those less capable would start in front while the real riders would start half a lap later, as they'd only catch up anyway, in fact they would thrash the others, winning every time. This continued until one evening Marco made a great race in the slipstream of the real riders, earning the right to start with them, half a lap behind. This was a great achievement for Marco; it was there that he began to realise that he could do this.
Then Panino came along and said: 'You see I was right?'

At that point we realised that set-up was also important and that we needed to work on the bike, the apprenticeship was almost over and if you wanted to keep up with the others you needed to be sorted. So we decided to start spending some money on this minibike and the first thing we did was buy a new clutch, we spent 100,000 lire I recall. The minibikes were all the same, and the clutch was the most important thing because they had continuously variable transmission...
Anyway, armed with our new clutch we prepared for Wednesday and got to Cattolica only to discover that they weren't doing the race anymore because it was September and the season was over!
The various regional Italian championships began in winter; minibikes

were at the height of their popularity at that time and were, I have to say, a great way to learn.

So we decided to go to Luca Pasini, Mattia's dad, who ran a minibike team together with his brother Maurizio. They put them together, running in every category: Junior A, Junior B, Junior C, Seniors and they had more than enough riders. He said he would take us, but at a price.

We needed to find a sponsor so we went to Uncle Giancarlo who owned a foundry in a nearby town. The San Clemente foundry was our first big sponsor, because Giancarlo went to the trouble of sponsoring the entire team. He and Pierpaolo Rossi helped us for two or three years, for as long as we raced minibikes. That was really the start, for Marco.

I gave in to you and your father's request to let you do the minibike championship. To be honest I would have preferred you not to do it but I thought about it and it seemed to me that nothing much would change and I would be denying you something that you enjoyed doing, perhaps causing you to resent me for saying no. I really hope you enjoy yourself, using balance, awareness, accuracy and responsibility. I will always love you, I tell you this repeatedly but I really do love you so much.

From Rossella's diary, 1996

DIRTY OIL STAINS

PAOLO The first official race was at Spoleto. I remember the excitement of that journey: we were in the black Mercedes 200E, all hyped up, first race, first trip, his mum was there too. We went down to Spoleto and when we arrived it was absolutely throwing it down but Marco wanted to ride anyway. The water on the track was 15 centimetres deep, enough to scare anyone, but he wanted to get out there at all costs. At that time Maurizio Pasini was always with Bianchi, an older rider in the Seniors category, and didn't have time for this young boy. He just said 'Go on', without even changing the tyres. Marco went out anyway on that soaking track with slick tyres... He starts off, first corner at the end of the straight, a 20-metre slide, he gets up absolutely drenched. He starts again, second corner, falls again. And again at the third corner. He finishes the lap and comes back to the garage alone... Anyway, Maurizio was a little careless, even Luca told him to put on rain tyres but he didn't, he totally blew him off. Later he too fell in love with Marco.

Anyway Marco always remembered the journey down to Spoleto for that race: he was so enthusiastic, poetic, with such expectations, it was wonderful. Zucchero's song, 'Cosi' celeste', was our soundtrack. Even now each time I hear that song it reminds me of that journey with the Mercedes 200E, the start of a great time for us.

Marco's sporting career began with that car that held out until it finally died. When he turned 18 Marco would take the Mercedes, with 560,000km on the clock, and go drifting. Then one day he called me: 'Um, dad, the car... I don't know, it won't go. What do I do?' 'Right, well call ACI... But what were you doing?' 'Nothing, it won't go.' I found out later that he had gone drifting and the engine had died. The roadside assistance guys brought the car back to the house and it stayed in the garage, he didn't want to sell it. We gave the plates back but Marco wanted to hold on to the car because he was really attached to his things, he never threw anything away. He even got the car fixed, so we still have the 200E in our garage, with no plates but in working condition. The boot is still full of dirty oil stains from all the trips we made with the minibike...

We had bought that car second-hand on Christmas Eve and for years it got us to all Marco's races, and I mean all of them. It wasn't like today where everyone has a camper; in those days you'd go to the minibike races by car, with the bikes in the boot. You'd get to the track, put up the stand, get the bike on the stand, toolbox out, and when the race was done you'd pack up and be off.

In Pasini's team there was also a boy from Cesena, Denis Sacchetti, who ran with number 58 as a matter of fact. His family had a camper. We got together and would always eat there with Laura, Denis's mum. We had some great years together.

Laura could see that her son wasn't at Marco's level; it couldn't have been easy for her. They spent a lot of time together and then on track Marco would make moves on Denis that couldn't have been easy for his mum to digest. They were also good friends with Dovizioso and his family. So you know what she would do? She'd tell Marco, while we were eating: 'Oh, you know what Dovizioso said?' Perhaps adding: 'You're slow', without realising that she was having the opposite effect because Marco would only become more determined. They thought they'd scare him or make him angry, make him go a bit slower but instead he'd push harder and become truly incredible.

1998

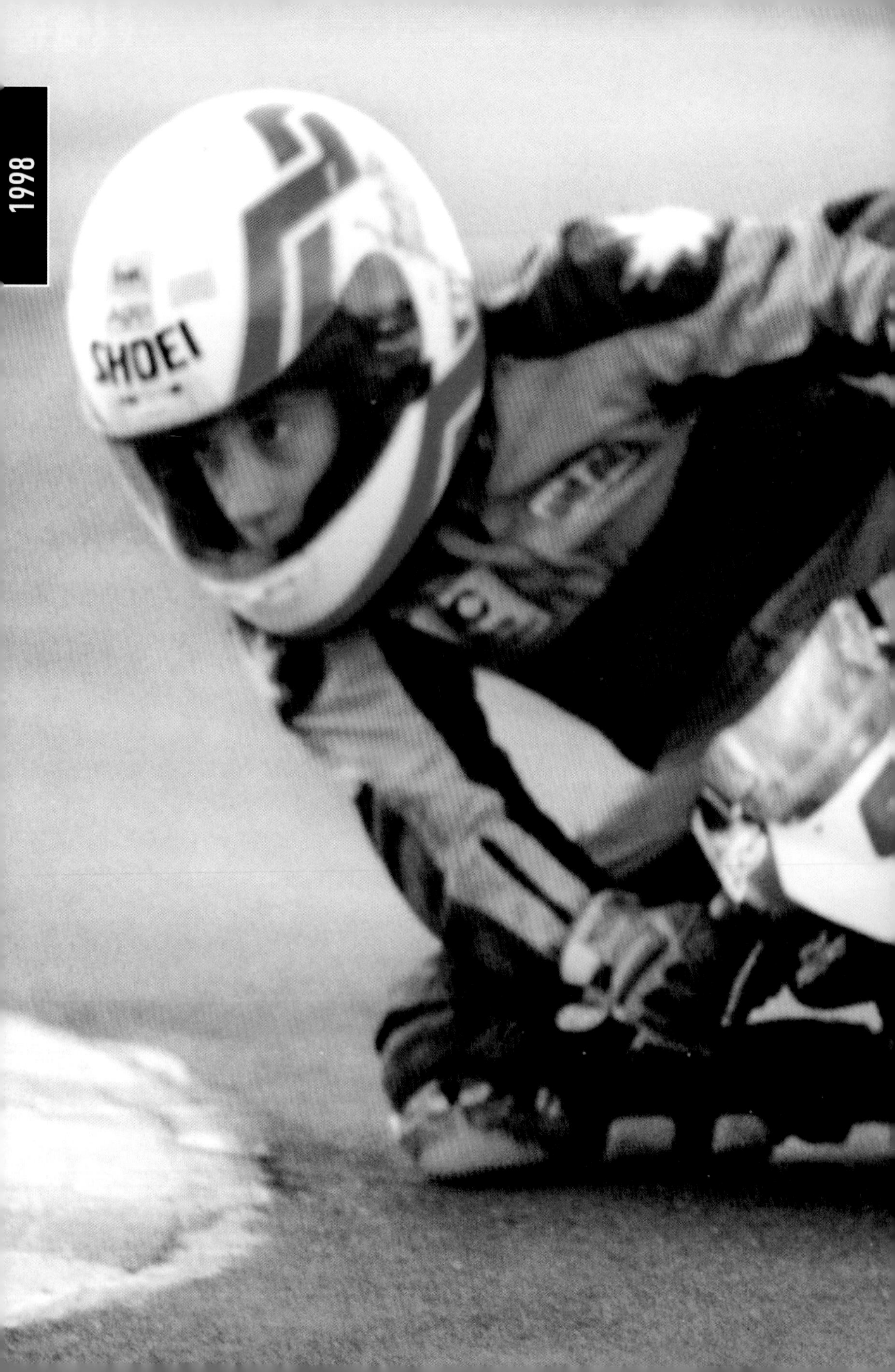

" TO KIDS THAT WANT TO START RACING, I'D SAY START WITH MINIBIKES, WHEN YOU'RE YOUNG YOU LEARN SO MUCH STUFF THERE. "

TRACTOR THIEVES

PAOLO In summer we were so busy, there was so much work at the ice-cream parlour from April until the end of September, and when Marco was small his grandparents were very important to him. He would help granddad Mario with the work in the fields: my dad would let him use the tiller in the vineyard and it was so funny to watch because he had the gall to teach Marco how to use the tractor... The only problem was that he wasn't the most capable himself. Marco also spent a lot of time with grandpa Italo and grandma Felicia, especially with his grandpa, he grew up with him. Sadly Italo passed away too soon; Marco got on so well with him and really felt the loss when he died, at school he wrote an essay that's still so touching to read now. Grandpa taught him many things, from how to use a lathe to how to steal a

tractor. 'But there's no key grandpa', 'You go underneath, disattach the wires, reattach them, the tractor starts and then you bring it here and make a lap, that way you work the land for me, OK?' Grandma would get annoyed: 'Italo, what on earth are you teaching him?' And he said, I remember this well: 'Oh let him dream...', and then he taught him to use the forklift. Grandpa would get on the forks and Marco would lift him to the top of the barn. Marco was three or four and grandma would get so mad you could hear her shouting all the way to Riccione!

He was a special grandpa and who knows, maybe Marco is with him right now... They say that when you die there's always a relative waiting to accompany you: for him it would surely have been grandpa Italo.

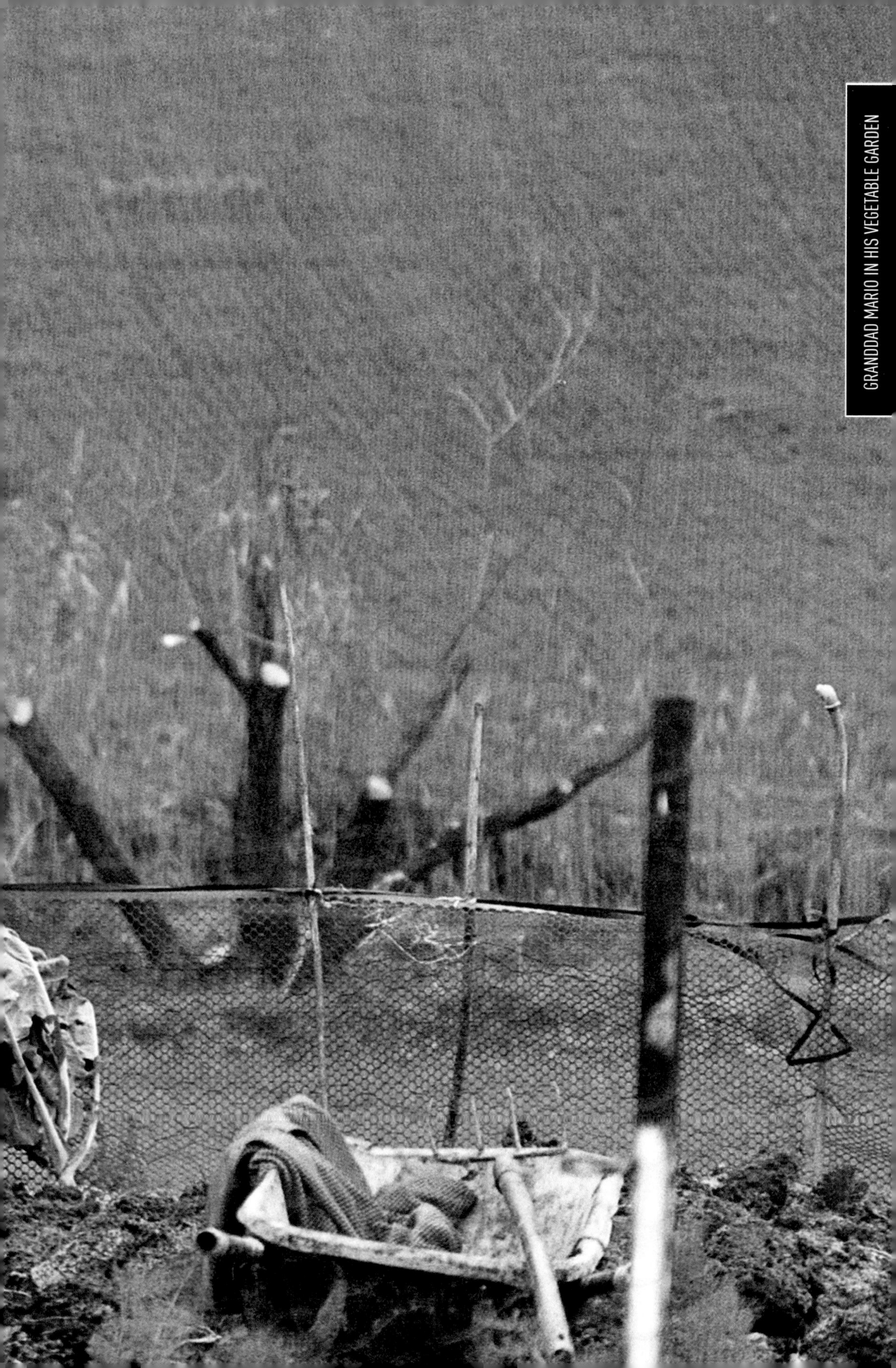

GRANDDAD MARIO IN HIS VEGETABLE GARDEN

A GREAT DREAM

One day I climbed a cherry tree, three or four metres high. I pushed myself onto a branch and began to think, daydream, fantasise.

As I daydreamed I realised I had a wish, hidden in the furthest corner of my heart, seemingly unattainable. I really wanted to spend another day together with grandpa Italo, who passed away on November 16 '94.

He taught me how to work the lathe, the forklift and many other machines in his workshop. In the evening, when we would sleep at his house, he would talk a lot about constellations, stars, comets, the force of gravity and loads of other things that I don't recall now.

Sometimes when I'm having trouble, like at school for example if I can't remember something, I have the impression that I can see him, a bit out of focus, and he talks to me and suggests things.

I see him in my room and I can see him for a second lying on the bed like he did when he would talk to me. In difficult moments I hear his voice and it consoles me.

So many memories still resurface now. When he'd take me to the park in the evening and we'd play together, when he'd let me move the forklift while he was on the forks, the countless times he'd take me for breakfast at the bar, and I can't forget those times he'd play cards with me and when he'd help me do my homework in the summer.

He really was a special grandpa, and now I miss him so, so much!

This wish to see him again only seems impossible because one day when I die, if I go to Heaven I will surely see him and will spend most of my time with him. When I see him the first thing I'll say will be: 'Grandpa, how have you managed without me all these years!!'

Marco Simoncelli, Riccione, 9 February 1998

“MY FIRST BIKE WAS A COLOURED PLASTIC THING BUT WITH A REAL ENGINE THAT MY PARENTS BOUGHT FOR ME. I ASKED AND ASKED UNTIL THEY GAVE IN. „

MAURIZIO PASINI   'THE WIND ENGINEER'

X MAURIZIO: L' INGEGNERE
DEL VENTO
CIAO !!

One day Paolo came to the workshop, he had this kid that wanted to race. We already had a good team: Poggiali, De Angelis, and then there was Mattia, my nephew, who rode a minibike and who Marco immediately viewed as a sort of example. Over the years this turned on its head and Mattia started to look to Marco as a model to follow.

MARCO HAD A GREAT WAY OF DOING THINGS; HE ALWAYS HAD GOOD RELATIONSHIPS WITH HIS TECHNICIANS. IT WAS NATURAL FOR HIM TO MAKE TIME FOR THOSE THAT WORKED WITH HIM, IT WAS A SORT OF GIFT HE HAD.

For example when you make changes to the bike and the rider comes in to say what he thinks about this and that, well some of them just say: 'Um, the bike doesn't work like this', while he would stay there with you and try to understand and he'd say: 'Mauri, for me it felt better before'. The way he behaved would reassure you, because he respected the work of the entire team.

When he was in the World Championship, one of his last years in 125, we bumped into each other in the street, he was cycling. We said hi and he said: 'Eh Mauri, when are you coming to a race with us? Go on, come!' 'Well if you're inviting me I'd love to', I replied. Two days later Paolo came by my house and said straight out: 'Marco told me you're coming with us!' I hesitated, 'Um, I don't know, I don't know...' But straight away he said: 'No, no, what Marco says is law', and that was how I ended up going with them to the next race.

Time passed so fast during the trips we made together. One time – Paolo and I had left by car to go to Brno in August 2009 – we went from Riccione up via the Brenner Pass and we ended up doing something like an extra 300km, but we didn't even realise it at the time! We only realised what a crazy route we had taken, making the trip so much longer, once we arrived... And that's because once we got into the car we started talking and didn't stop until we got there! It was in Brno that we took our last photograph together. It was his first GP podium. Aligi Deganello and Malabrocca were there with us. Marco had just got changed and said: 'Come on Mauri, let's take a historic photo with all my technicians'. And he hugged us.

Simoncelli rules

> " WHEN THE FIRST 140KPH
> WINS COME (THAT'S HOW IT IS
> WHEN YOU'RE 11!) YOU FORGET
> EVERYTHING; THE TIREDNESS, THE
> TRAVELLING, THE SACRIFICES DON'T
> COUNT ANY MORE, NOT EVEN FOR
> THE MUMS. AND YOU ARE SO HAPPY
> THAT ALL YOU WANT IS TO CONTINUE
> DOING THE THING THAT YOU FEEL
> YOU WERE BORN TO DO: RACE! "

The evening he won the 250 championship I sent him a message. I wrote: 'Marco, you remember that time we went to do that race at Altivole? And we saw Noale and I asked you if I should turn off? Thanks to you I feel a bit like a World Champion too'.

To explain the message: we were in the car, he was still a kid, we got to Altivole, stopped at a light and I saw the sign for Noale – where Aprilia has its base – and so I asked him: 'What should I do Marco, shall I turn?' He started laughing and I went straight.

I remember that after he got my message he called me to say: 'Mauri, that was one of the best messages I've received'.

MAURIZIO PASINI	IT CAN'T RAIN EVERY SUNDAY

The first race that he did with us was at Spoleto, one Saturday afternoon, and it was throwing it down with rain. He and Paolo had arrived late, having hit traffic, but they wanted to test the track anyway.

At that point I said to them: 'Paolo, look it's useless riding in this, he'll do two laps and won't stay upright'.

And what happened? With slick tyres Marco made two laps and fell five times. Five. But what could you say to him?

HE WOULD NEVER BACK DOWN BECAUSE HE HAD THAT WILL TO RACE, ALWAYS, AND ÀS WELL AS THE WILL THERE WAS ALSO HIS THICK HEAD.

At a race in Giulianova, again during the first year, I saw him come in under the tent crying and he said to his dad: 'They're telling me that Dovizioso and Cornacchia – two racers who had started the year before so they were a bit more crafty – want to knock me off'.

So I told him how something very similar had happened to my brother Luca when he was racing motocross: a Roman rider had told him that someone wanted to stress him out and make him crash. In reality it was him, the Roman, who had invented the whole thing to scare him and trick him! And the next day, as the race started, Marco was off like a bulldozer, leaving the guy who was trying to provoke him behind, because he had listened to the story that I'd told him and he'd understood how things sometimes work.

When he won his first race in the wet, he came to me and said: 'Mauri, I rode like Angelo.' He meant like Angelo Costantini, one of the team, older than Marco, who would never lose a race in the wet. He would win because he'd keep the bike upright and lean over very little, unlike Marco.

One time we went to test rain tyres, one made specifically for minibikes and one suitable for karts. 'But it's impossible that the kart tyre is better,' I told myself, 'Marco leans a lot, he'll never stay up.' We went to Gatteo Mare to do the test, it was raining but as soon as we got there it stopped. So we took the car and headed towards Cattolica, where it was thrashing down, so much so that that evening they talked of cloudbursts on the news. We started to lap and in the end we were all left surprised because the kart tyres performed better, with Marco lapping and lapping, he never stopped!

He really liked riding in the wet, he'd always say to me:

'BUT I NEED TO LEARN TO GO FAST IN THE DRY TOO BECAUSE, GOOD LORD, IT CAN'T RAIN EVERY SUNDAY!'

LUCA PASINI	A PICNIC WITH ENGINES

When minibikes first came out they were the best way to get into the world of motorcycling from a young age, and for years they helped build champions. Now it's all changed, they've divided the selections, kids don't make as many sacrifices in order to make it. My fear is that they're no longer born here: a boxer for example doesn't come from a rich world; he needs to come from a certain context where you come to blows over a piece of bread. It's not like we were living in poverty but we still had the passion that pushed us to say: 'Regardless of what I have, I must give it my all.'

THE KIDS SAW THE RACES AS A GAME, AND THAT'S HOW IT SHOULD BE.

Then, over time, it can become a profession but inside it should always remain a joy, an enjoyable thing. It's important for children: if they learn to never give up, then they will get on in life regardless of what they end up doing, motorcycling or not – that, there, is the character that they hold inside forever.

I have seen kids on other teams cry because they finished second, because someone had put it into their heads that second means 'first loser'... things like that never happened with us, precisely because everything should become an incentive to improve.

THIS SPORT WAS LIKE A GAME AMONG FRIENDS FOR US, A WEEKEND SPENT TOGETHER, LIKE A SORT OF PICNIC WITH ENGINES.

A country outing at the tracks, where the competition continued to grow because winning was the goal, as winning meant an adrenalin surge and incredible satisfaction.

Taking the car to races would become a tale in itself, like that time that we were coming back from a race and got lost in the hills around Covignano. It was the Sunday before Ferragosto, traffic was insane, so instead of getting stuck in line on the autostrada we decided to exit at Rimini Nord and take the internal road. We ended up covering a lot more miles by getting lost in the hills, as if we were 2,000km from home. And the fact is that as we passed over the many flyovers we saw that the autostrada was almost deserted... these are the things that help to downplay the tension that comes with race days.

Marco, regardless of the condition of the bike he was riding, would always give 100 per cent, and always with a smile on his face. He was one of those riders that, even in warm-up, would bring me a bike that was in bits because perhaps he had tried to improve something and I knew that I shouldn't reprimand him, I knew that this was the only way to push the limit further – by trying and trying again.

HE DEFINITELY WASN'T SCARED OF ANYTHING OR ANYBODY, HE HAD NO DOUBT IN HIS ABILITIES, NOT EVEN WHEN HE FINISHED BEHIND OR FELL, HE KNEW THAT HE HAD GIVEN IT HIS ALL, THAT HE HAD FOUGHT.

And this is what made the difference in Marco, it's undeniable. He thirsted after finesse, strategy. When we spoke about champions, riders of the time like Gardner or Spencer, he would absorb everything; he would learn tricks like touching the brakes mid-turn to put his adversary on edge. Marco always put everything he learned into practice.

Every time that we headed to races on a Saturday or Sunday we'd come across the trucks that transport horses. So with Marco we invented this: 'Warning, boy racers on board'.

Marco and I started racing together as children. We were all friends, there was Pellino, Lai, Dovizioso... Then we met up again in the World Championship. Marco was an official Pasini rider, I was with Polini and Dovizioso with CRC, so we were always rivals, even though he was a bit older than me and changed category a year before me. I remember that there was a bit of friction between Dovizioso and Simoncelli because Marco was always like that: he'd always go up the inside of you. Later on Marco continued to have great rivalry with different riders, but I think he had his own particular riding style, due to his physique. Even as a kid that had always been his strength, he'd push in, even if there was no space, he'd get straight to the point. It didn't bother me too much, because great races are like that: if you need to push you do it, if you need to take him you take him and in the next race he gets you back. That's how it was, and then there were those who would take a little more and those who would accept it.

We were team-mates in Gilera in 2006, and I was comfortable there. Marco enjoyed it. He had some difficult times but he was always a cheerful guy, strong, and his dad was always there with him. He achieved what he did because he always believed and always gave it everything. He had grown a lot: 'ifs' unfortunately don't count but he would have rewritten the history of MotoGP.

The minibike championships were between us two. Others tried too but we were always the most motivated, even when we were kids. Winning was our only thought. The difference is that if he didn't win he'd laugh about it. He'd get mad but never lost his smile, and the next race he'd go faster. I, on the other hand, would cry, total desperation, for me being beaten was the end of the world. Basically we had totally different approaches. Mine was studied: you understand, and then you push. His: you throw yourself into it, crash and then try to learn. Maybe it takes a year but you understand that way, by running headlong at it.

WHATEVER HE DID, MARCO WOULD FALL AND GET UP STRONGER THAN BEFORE.

With a bit of luck...
San Mauro 1999

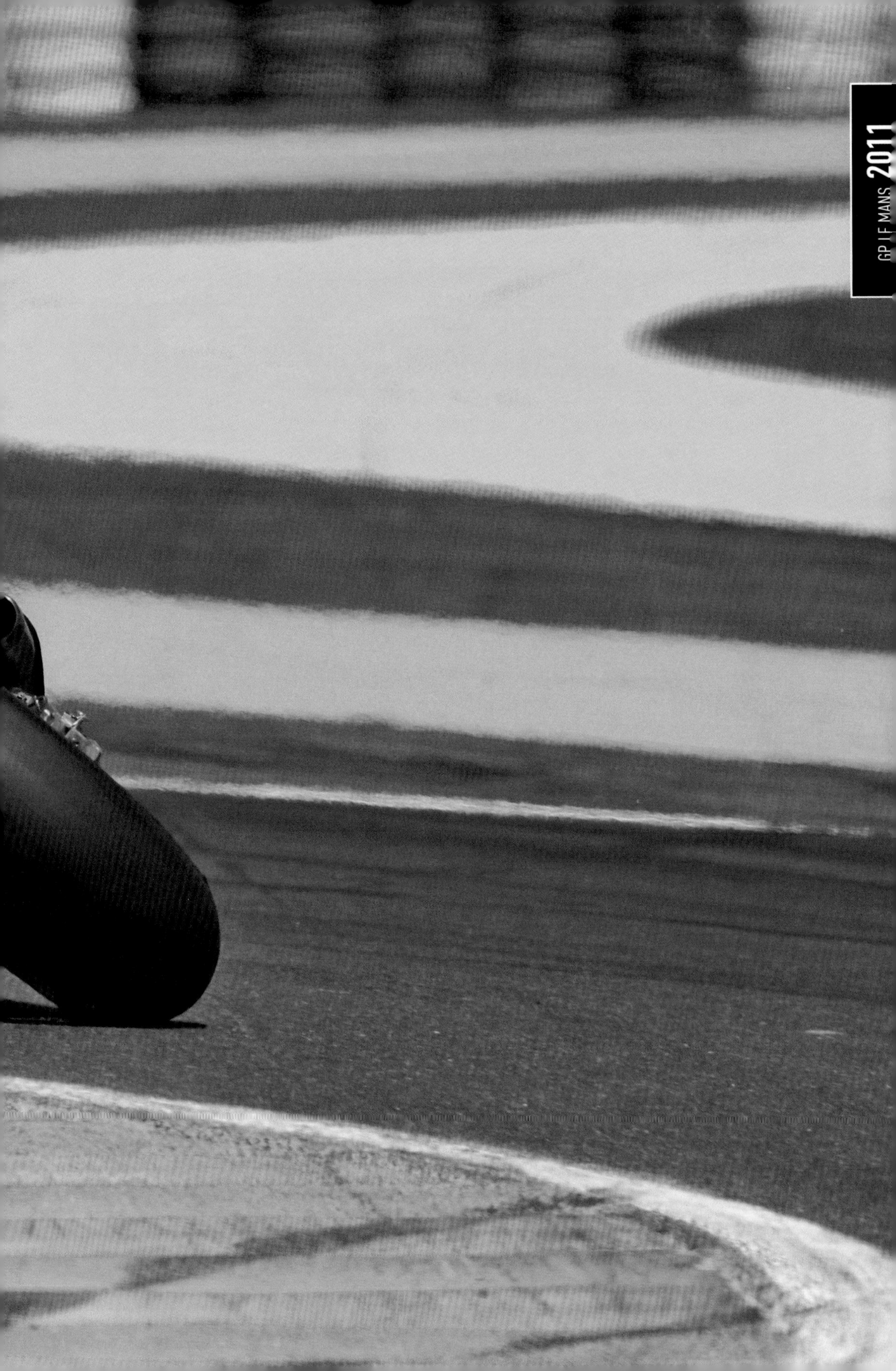

SPORT AND ME

My favourite sport is minibike racing, I chose it because I have a passion for motorsport and my father passed this passion on to me, in fact, when I was small, he would do nothing but talk to me about the great riders in the World Championship and engines.

I race in the 'Pasini mini project racing' team which is supported financially by the 'Fonderia San Clemente', 'Moca' and the 'Ina Assitalia' insurance company.

Sometimes I get depressed because other riders are faster than me, but the managers of the team, Luca Pasini and Maurizio Pasini, take care of cheering me up. They are very nice, they always want to joke and know how to encourage all the riders in the team. I get on well with them and really feel at home.

My dad doesn't make sacrifices to take me racing, in fact he enjoys it because he is a huge petrol-head and he likes seeing me on the track. My mum on the other hand has never been interested in engines and does it for me; she always laughs and jokes with the other mums, which relieves the boredom. When I train I try new parts and so, while I'm lapping, I have to try and feel whether the change that the mechanics have made has improved performance or made it worse, so when I'm riding it's not much fun.

Before I start I'm really nervous but when the green light goes on all my nerves fade away. Often when I win or get a great result I feel huge satisfaction and the first time I passed the chequered flag in first position I nearly cried. Sometimes however this sport leaves me very disappointed, for example, when the bike breaks during a race or when I crash and throw away a whole championship.

I hope to become a future Eddie Lawson or even Valentino Rossi and I think I have what it takes.

Marco Simoncelli, Riccione, 10 December 1997

2. JUST US

A GUY WITH CURLY HAIR

It was 2006, I was 17. I was with a friend in Viale Ceccarini in Riccione, handing out flyers for the nightclubs. From a distance I saw two guys, one had curly hair and the other was really hot. So I said to my friend: 'I'm going over to them.' I got over there and said: 'Villa delle Rose?' to the hot one. The curly-haired one took my flyer and replied: 'Yeah, if you come too.' I took the flyer back and said: 'But I was inviting your friend!' The friend was Fuzzi and I gave him the flyer. Fuzzi laughed and Marco quickly said: 'Look, he has a girlfriend.' With those few words he cut him down. And Fuzzi said: 'What's it got to do with you, mind your own business Simoncelli!'

A couple of days later he called me: 'I'm taking you to eat fish in a nice restaurant.' 'I hate fish.' 'Just like that, come on! 'Ok, then I'll take you for a steak dinner in a nice restaurant.' 'Look, I'm here to spend time with my girl friends, I have a boyfriend in Bergamo, I don't want to go out with you.'

Slam, I hung up.

A few evenings later I bumped into him by chance. Because he was interested in me he wasn't taking any notice of other girls but at a certain point he left the bar and a girl jumped on him. How are you, what's going on, they probably knew each other by sight, he looked at her and said: 'Listen, until Saturday at 4pm I'm going out with her, after that I'm all yours. Ciao!'

That evening we got on well, perhaps he finished one of my sentences and I went:

'Oh, stop it won't you?' And he said: 'No! Don't you see we're made for each other?' 'Oh yeah, sure, he's the one!' I think I won him over mentally rather than physically. He said he would get bored after half an hour with other girls.

On the Saturday I left and we didn't see each other for a while, but a few days later he called me: 'I'm in Milan, at my cousins' place.' I wanted to introduce him to my dad because he likes the bike world. But to be sure Marco wouldn't get any strange ideas, I told him straight: 'Come with us to the lake because my dad wants to meet you but, look, I only see you as a friend, I have a boyfriend and I'm keeping him.'

He came to the lake anyway, met my dad, he had this face, his eyes were shining as I introduced them and then Marco went home. Some days later my boyfriend found out that Simoncelli was at Lago d'Iseo with a certain Kate. The gossip mill had reached his place and his best friend had told him: 'I heard that Simoncelli was with a girl from Bagnatica who goes to Lago d'Iseo, it looks like it's Kate...'

So he rang me, I was asleep. 'Did Simoncelli like the lasagne?'

'Why?' I asked him, a bit mad.

'Because! Do I need to tell you it's over or is this call enough?'

Slam! He hung up on me.

Great. My boyfriend pretty much cast me off right there.

Apart from a couple of weeks of indecisiveness, in which I said: 'Look, nothing happened', lying unashamedly because there had been a kiss in the meantime, in Riccione. 'Come on... We didn't do anything; I just wanted to introduce him to my dad.' In the meantime I wrote to Marco: 'Look, that's it for me, I can't even keep you as a friend because my boyfriend is mad.' And he replied with one of those sweet messages, and I was really upset.

I tried to talk to my mum about it, but she said: 'You don't understand anything.' Just like that, because she didn't like the guy, while she really liked Marco, straight away: exuberant, fun... The other one would never talk, sometimes he wouldn't even take his sunglasses off, so as soon as my parents met a nice, sweet boy with another way of doing things, my mum immediately put her oar in: 'Come on, he's a good person, he's a good kid.'

I said: 'Yes, a good person, a rider, come on, we wouldn't last a month in a long-distance relationship, Riccione–Bergamo...' Apart from the fact he was a rider, I didn't believe that guys from Riccione could be with a girl seriously. My mum continued to push: 'Give him a chance at least.'

Instead I wrote to him saying enough was enough, that I didn't care about him and didn't want to see him again. He was upset, he replied saying that he was really cut up about it. So partly due to my mum and partly due to him – after two weeks he hadn't stopped contacting me – when he told me he was going to see his cousin in Milan, I used it as an excuse to see him. Ricky made me laugh that evening: 'Marco, we used to see you twice a year maybe, why is it you're up here every two weeks now?'

We got to a bar in Milan, it was the first time I met Ricky and it was just the three of us. Ricky kept getting out these tokens that you use to get drinks. He had loads of them and at a certain point we were so drunk that we were throwing them around. The key moment of the evening, I continued to tell Marco: 'No, it's no good. I only see you as a friend, I don't want to do anything with you and one more caipiroska won't push me to do something I don't want to do.' And then later that evening we ended up in bed together...

Ricky created another scene when he ended up in a fight with a guy because he had whispered in a girl's ear that: 'I would fuck you better than your boyfriend.' All while the boyfriend was standing there. The guy lashed out, ready to hit him, but in the end nothing happened, I don't know who broke that one up.

That same evening we were sleeping at Ricky's place. Marco parked up, pulled the hand brake, something went wrong and bang! We hit the neighbour's wall. The neighbour came out in his pants. Ricky's dad came down too: they were both in their pants. Ricky's dad assured the neighbour: 'We're so sorry, we'll sort it out tomorrow. Goodnight.' They'd totally broken his wall! There was also a road sign with the pole all bent. And a broken suspension arm. The next day Marco got up and started going: 'No, Ricky, I can't ring my dad, I'm not well.' He kept chanting it, until his continuous complaining woke me up...

I looked at him and said: 'Come on, how bad can it be?'

And him: 'But I've broken the suspension arm three times.'

It was August. And Ricky was laughing because he could imagine Paolo's reaction. Marco said: 'What can I say to him?'

And Ricky: 'That a wall crossed the street in front of you!'

'Fuck off...' Marco was desperate. 'No, I can't do it; I'll tell him it was raining.'

And Ricky: 'Tell him it was raining, he won't believe you anyway.'

An hour later he finally managed to pick up the phone: 'Oh dad, I can't get back.... Because it was a bit wet, I skidded; I pulled the hand brake and broke the arm... Um.'

And Paolo: 'What the fuck!'

I started to get to know Paolo right then... We'd met for the first time at a race at Valencia. Paolo took me trackside for the practices and because he's superstitious and saw that Marco was doing well, I was obliged to stay trackside for qualifying too. He sees me, he takes me out there for the race as well and what does Marco do? He falls. I didn't bring such good luck!

My father had come too and I told him: 'Simoncelli's dad is stuck up.' And he said: 'No, he's not stuck up, it's just that he's got things to do, he's under pressure, come on, try to understand.' Actually I would never have imagined the pressure; I would only understand that the following year.

At the start she didn't pay me much attention

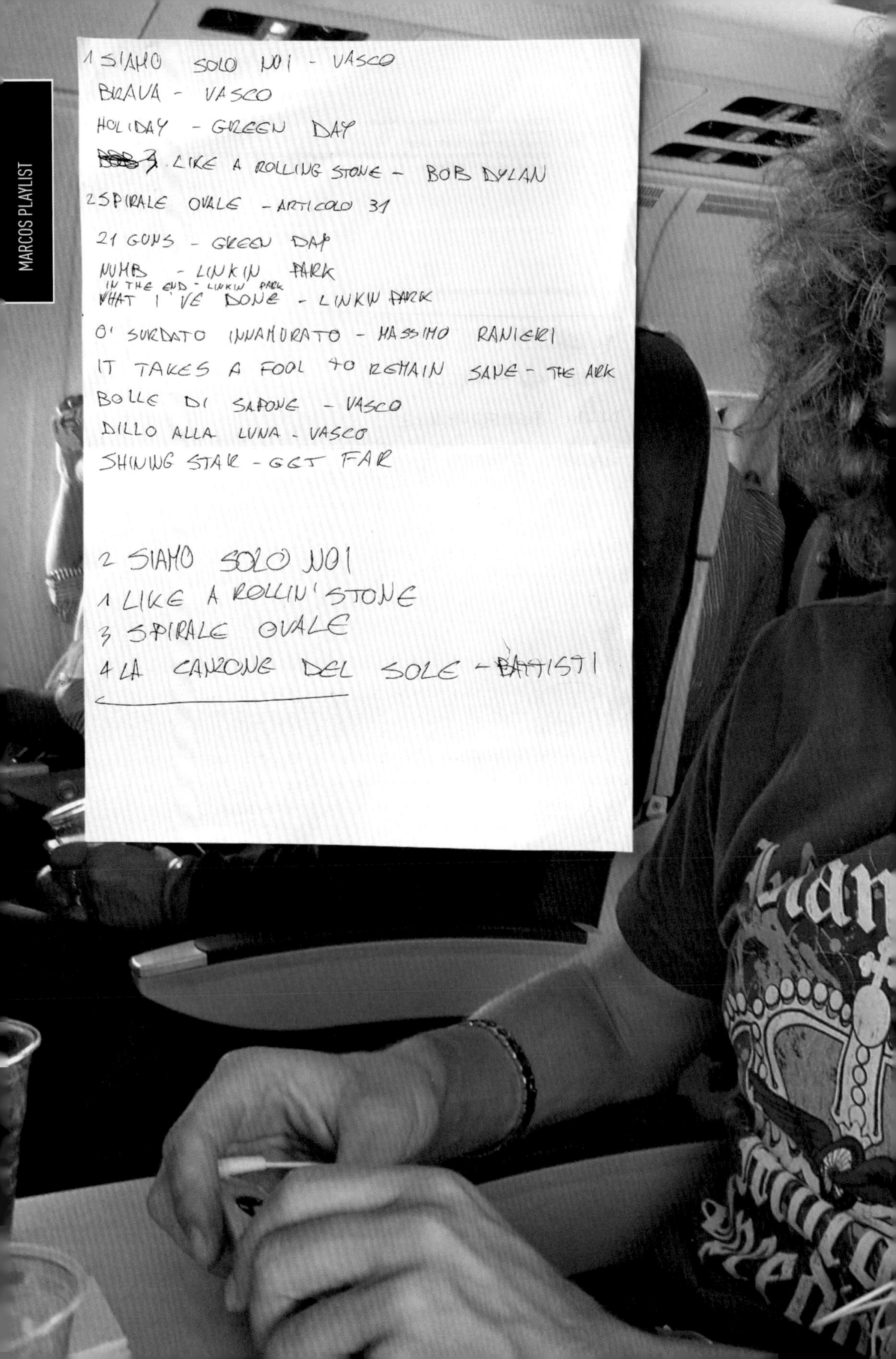

1 SIAMO SOLO NOI - VASCO
BRAVA - VASCO
HOLIDAY - GREEN DAY
~~BOB~~ LIKE A ROLLING STONE - BOB DYLAN
2 SPIRALE OVALE - ARTICOLO 31
21 GUNS - GREEN DAY
NUMB - LINKIN PARK
IN THE END - LINKIN PARK
WHAT I'VE DONE - LINKIN PARK
O' SURDATO INNAMORATO - MASSIMO RANIERI
IT TAKES A FOOL TO REMAIN SANE - THE ARK
BOLLE DI SAPONE - VASCO
DILLO ALLA LUNA - VASCO
SHINING STAR - GGI FAR

2 SIAMO SOLO NOI
1 LIKE A ROLLIN' STONE
3 SPIRALE OVALE
4 LA CANZONE DEL SOLE - BATTISTI

I like all kinds of girls, it depends on the moment

Marco never officially asked me to be his girlfriend. One day at Valencia he introduced me to his crew chief, Brazzi: 'Um, this is my girlfriend.'

I looked at him a bit strangely, but it was rude to reply: 'No, it's not true', so I simply introduced myself, what could I do? But then I said to Marco: 'Don't you ask me things first?' and he said: 'Haha, I put you in a position where you couldn't say no.' Well fuck you! And he went on: 'I knew you weren't enough of a bitch to say "No, it's not true" and so I said it, and now you can't change your mind.'

So, we'd been together for a day when this Dutch girl showed up the following evening. I didn't do a thing because I didn't even have time to realise, and anyway I wasn't jealous, if anything I might have been angry because he was there with me. If it had been the year after, I would have head butted her but instead when she came along, bye bye. So she sent him a message: 'Where are you? I'm at the bar' and he said to me: 'You answer her, in English' and so I wrote: 'We're coming.' We got to the bar and instead of giving him three kisses on the cheek she stuck her tongue down his throat and he said: 'Uh, sorry, sorry, I'm here with her.' And she, furious, said: 'So why the fuck were you looking for me?' and he went: 'But it was you who came looking for me'...

At the end of the evening it's usually the rider who takes you home... or not. I had to go with him to the track in a taxi then head back to the hotel because I had an early flight. There was this funny episode as I left him and starting heading off:

'No, I know we won't see each other again...'

And me: 'But why Marco? You're being paranoid.'

Basically drinking had made him sad.

'No, I know we won't see each other again.' He was desperate.

'Come on, you'll make me miss my plane.'

'No, come on, stay, sleep here Kate!'

'No, I'm not staying here and sleeping in the camper with your dad! Are you kidding?'

And then he said to me: 'I have to tell you something.'

And me: 'Jeez, don't say it, you're drunk, I know what you're going to say...'

'I love you.'

'Oh god, you've only known me a month!' I was panicking, 'Marco, stop it.' And he goes: 'Yes, yes, I can feel it.'

I kicked him out of the taxi and left.

One month later he was already saying: 'I'm taking you to meet my parents as my mum hasn't ever seen you.'

And me: 'Oh shit!'

Trying to be cool he took all the small roads, not the normal one. He was purposely looking for the narrowest road because he wanted me to shit myself while he drove like a bat out of hell. He went over a tiny bridge between the fields, you couldn't see over the other side. Thank god he knew the road, he took it at full speed and I kept on thinking: 'Now we're going to roll over...' But of course I didn't let on. He must have been doing 90kph, then he threw it right, I didn't know there was a road there!

'Are you nuts?'

And he goes: 'Fantastic! I love bringing people home for the first time!'

Ok... As soon as we arrived he told his parents about taking that road at 90kph. I think they liked me, and the best bit was that two days after I left Marco told me: 'Martina has written "I miss Kate" on her door.'

CARLO CASABIANCA — **AT THE BUOY**

He cared so much for Kate, because... well, after the World Championship there were several girls lining up ready to screw him and we tried hard to talk him into it but he always resisted. Even at the gym there were two or three girls that would hassle him and each of us gave him some advice. I told him: 'Marco, if you really like Kate don't cheat on her. You can joke around, talk about it, but don't do it'.

I remember exactly when he met her. One day, it was right when he first started going out with her, he came to the gym and said: 'Good lord, I've met this girl from Bergamo, I took her out in the water to the buoy...' Basically, he told us how he'd screwed her out at the buoy and we went: 'Shit, well done Sic... At the buoy!' When we saw Kate we would always look at her with respect, the girl who agreed to be screwed at the buoy... But it wasn't even true.

KATE — **AT THE BUOY**

We'd been together about a year, I was at Carlo's gym and, laughing and joking, he tells me that everyone knew about me and Marco shagging at the buoy. In reality Marco and I had been at the beach that day, we'd only been together a short time and we'd only kissed at the buoy.

'But, sorry, who told you that?' And he said: 'Marco!' So I went to him and said: 'Marco, but what have you been telling people?' 'No, why, at the buoy, come on, didn't I shag you there?'

'No, it's not true!' Carlo came over and said: 'What do you mean no, you told me a year ago Sic!' 'Oh, OK, more or less, I gave her a limoncino'. And Carlo goes: 'It's not the same thing! For a year and a half you've been showing off about screwing a girl at the buoy and it's not even true!'

> **"THEY TOOK MY LICENCE OFF ME AFTER TWO DAYS BUT I WAS LUCKY BECAUSE, SEEING AS THEY'D TAKEN IT FROM ME IN SAN MARINO, AT LEAST I COULD STILL DRIVE IN ITALY."**

KATE	DRIVING SCHOOL

When we got together I didn't yet have my driving licence and so Marco gave me lessons... My dad certainly wasn't going to teach me how to swerve between the cones, first, second, third lane. Yes, he might have taught me to flash my lights at the guy in front or to push him into overtaking but not to swerve between the cones.

So anyway, drifting, things like that, I miss doing them. And no-one except Mattia Pasini has a car with rear-wheel drive nowadays. Now and then I use the handbrake, when it's wet: you drive up to the roundabout, in second, dip the clutch and then quickly come off it, the rear wheels lock, give a little throttle, and the car slides sideways. Then hard on the throttle and make it turn, until the tyres burst or become bald.

When there were tyres to finish off, Paolo would go to Marco and say: 'Look, in three days we need to change the tyres.' And he'd go: 'Ok, I'll go and finish them off on the industrial estate.'

One time, it was 2007, he was teaching me to start the motorino. 'Come on, you try,' he says. 'OK,' I replied. I got on the front, he got off.

'What are you doing?' I said.

'Oh, I'm going to the camper, I don't want to hurt myself, I've got a race.'

'Are you crazy?' The motorino weighed more than me!

And he just said: 'Go on, try it, do a couple of stops, and if you need a hand call me.'

Ok, so I needed a hand, because of course I fell, I was asking for it. A guy had to come and help me as I couldn't even get the motorino on the stand.

I went to Marco, pissed off: 'Jesus, you were supposed to come and help me' and he's there with his feet on the table, reading *Motosprint*, and he said: 'Uh, why, did you call me?'

"I'VE RENEWED MY CONTRACT WITH KATE ONCE AGAIN THIS YEAR."

KATE	GIFTS

During the last year when we made a bet we would bet gifts, so if I won he had to buy me a gift. If he won I had to get him something, anything, but it couldn't just be a chocolate bar. But it couldn't be a car either. Of course he could have got me a car, but I couldn't do the same for him.

One time, I'd been working for a month and I was in crisis because I didn't like my job. I only had three days off because they didn't close down for Christmas and then he told me that he wasn't coming up to Bergamo. 'But hang on, I only have three days off and we won't even be together for those three days.' Maybe I could have reacted differently but in that moment I wasn't thinking straight and I started to cry. 'Because you're a shit', all guns firing, I could sense he was starting to soften. 'No, come on, maybe I can make it.' That afternoon the doorbell rang, I opened it to find him there. It was a great surprise, better than many other gifts.

In September I had stopped taking the pill because I was having a few problems. 'Look, I've got to go and get the coil,' I told him, 'it would be a disaster if we had a kid now...'

He didn't flinch, actually he said: 'It just means he'd have young parents.'

'Yeah, OK,' I said, 'But we still want to go out and party, not stay here with a child!' And he said: 'Come on, shit, how great would it be to have a kid now, in 12 years he and I could go around on the motocross bike together!' Typical. And so I said to him: 'I get it, so if it's a boy you're happy but if it's a girl what then? I kick her because you wanted a boy? Thanks!'

Then, when Marco had the accident, I hoped for a moment to be pregnant. To have something of his... But, if you think about having your whole life ahead of you, a girl doesn't have a child at 22...

A journalist once asked me: 'Don't you have any regrets?' And I replied: 'Look, if I was 30, and what had happened had happened, I'd have no doubt and I'd tell you that my biggest regret was not having got married, not having a child. But at 22 we did what we could.' Shit, we were even going to move in together, that was already huge...

" AND NOW GAS! "

MARCO BEFORE MARCO

PAOLO The story of my son started long before 20 January 1987. I think Marco's story began when I was dating one of Rossella's friends and then met her. We were together for a year, a year and a half, and when they offered me a job in Naples Rossella agreed to this adventure and came to live with me, even though we weren't married. This wasn't easy, we're talking about 30 years ago.

The Naples experience came to an end when the owner of the company died in the Ustica plane crash and the company fell apart. At that point we returned home and bought our first ice-cream parlour. We were still not married but I had got Rossella to sign 200 or 300 million lire's worth of promissory notes... We had so many debts but it was different to how it is today, there was opportunity to work and paying back debts wasn't a problem.

After a while we started making money but when we began to think about having a child we found we were unsuccessful: as with anything, when you really want something it doesn't arrive. We tried for a couple of years and then we decided to start the process of visiting doctors to understand what was wrong. I remember well, we fixed the appointment for 10 June and in May Rossella fell pregnant!

It was 1986. The year of the Chernobyl disaster and at that point doctors started to tell us we should abort because no-one knew the range of the radiation. We went to different doctors and they all told us the same thing. Rossella and I looked each other in the eye and decided to continue. We would have accepted anything.

As always he was in a hurry, just as he was throughout his whole life, and he was born a month early. I wasn't in the delivery room, because I'm convinced that that particular moment is for the mother alone. I saw Marco for the first time as they took him to the incubator. They quickly passed by and I only saw two things: that he had a deformed head, all rippled! And then I was struck by his... willy. He had an enormous penis! They kept him in an incubator for one night and then he was OK on his own. Sometimes it seems that those born prematurely become stronger and more robust, for him it was like that.

Choosing a name was easy, much easier than it would be later with Martina. Lucio Dalla had that song of his, 'Anna e Marco', and it was so full of sentiment that we decided to name him after that: 'Marco, big shoes, skinny body...' That was him to a tee.

DIARY ENTRIES

'Where did you come from?'
your father asked you.
Answer: 'From a seed with "special" written on it.
And it was mummy who pointed it out to you saying:
"It's that one, that one is the right one."'

From Rossella's diary, 1995

ROSSELLA I have so many of these diaries; it was a gift that I wanted to present to Marco once he was an adult. Actually I wrote somewhere that: 'These diaries will be a gift from me to you. It will be a rather special gift', and as I wrote it I choked up. Now I choke up even more. He never even read a page. As I reread certain sections I realise that, even after two, three years, I would have forgotten these things. But instead it's wonderful to see them written down. I'm so happy I did it.

Marco's school diaries however never went further than December. He would fill the pages with signatures, because he needed to learn to sign his autograph. At one point the autograph had a star, and then eventually he came up with the final version. He would sign everywhere. I don't know whether they still have those desks covered with his signatures at school...

MARTINA

'Mummy, where do babies come from?'
Answer: 'From mummy's tummy.'
Question: 'And how do they get into her tummy?'
Answer: 'From the sexual relations between the man
and the woman.'
'But then you're really lacking!'
A moment of confusion in my mind, my answers
perhaps weren't satisfactory. I risk asking why.
And you: 'You only made me!'

From Rossella's diary, 1995

ROSSELLA Marco always complained that, in his class, he was alone in being an only child while everyone else had brothers or sisters. He had wanted it so much and finally he got a sister. He was already eleven, so there was a big age difference but he was in seventh heaven.

Marco was already away at weekends because he was doing the minibike championship, and up until then I had always gone with him. Once Martina was born I had a bit more trouble. But it was great when Marco would leave – not just for the races, even if he was only going to a friend's place – as he would give me advice: 'Mum, have you seen Martina? She's here, OK?', 'Mum, remember Martina.' He was really protective over his little sister.

While Martina was in primary school we would often all go to Marco's races together, even though it meant she'd miss school, to be honest we took advantage. Then once she was at middle school it was more difficult to miss school, and also she would get bored at a track all day. I enjoyed it, her not so much. But then in the final years, maybe because she would go less often, maybe because she was older, she started to enjoy it too, to be interested. She even did some sketches dedicated to Marco that Aldo Drudi decided to include as part of Marco's helmet design.

Last year, during summer, Marco was playing football with his friends at the sports field in Riccione and Paolo, Martina and I showed up. One of Marco's friends told me that he went up to Marco to ask: 'So who's that, is that Kate?' We were a way away, he couldn't see well. And he goes: 'No, that's my sister and don't even look at her.' Basically the typical jealousy and protectiveness of the older brother was beginning!

They started to get on well, because it's one thing to be three and 14 but another to be 14 and 24. Something beautiful was beginning to grow between them, they could almost see eye to eye.

Until then they had always teased each other mercilessly. He was really a pain in the neck and she would never back down – because he would never back down – so there were rows from morning till night. One day, shortly after Martina was born, Marco came to us and said: 'Jeez, this one's only just been born and already half the house is hers!'

One time we were all together in the mountains and Martina had started to ski well. Paolo and I watched her come down and we said: 'Marco, did you see how well Martina's doing?' And he goes: 'Hmm, I was much better than her at that age!' He wouldn't accept it! And when she was in the third year at school and was learning her times tables, Paolo would test her with the chronometer in his hand, to make it more fun. Marco was 19, he would stop whatever he was doing in his room and come down to 'compete' against his eight-year-old sister. We would hear thump thump thump down the stairs and then: 'Me too! Come on dad, me too!'

WHERE DID THIS ONE COME FROM?

ROSSELLA Kate and Marco weren't one of those clingy couples, far from it! Totally different. I always admired this about them: they lived far apart and in addition she was at school, then at work, and was busy all week. They only had the weekends when either Marco would go to her or she'd come here. I sometimes got upset because she'd come down, on the Friday evening or Saturday afternoon, and he'd head off to the Cava! But she wouldn't get angry and didn't get upset: maybe we'd go and do some shopping in town, her and me. Kate is extraordinary; she was always extraordinary and important to him, right from the moment they met, in 2006, when Marco was going through a difficult time.

The first time she came here, Paolo and I looked at each other and said: 'Where did this one come from?' It was the first time she'd come to this house, I thought she might feel a little awkward, you know, going to see the boyfriend's parents... But it was like she'd always been here; she was very polite, she moved around with nonchalance as if she'd always lived here. You saw her there, in her pyjamas, relaxed... And she wasn't even 18! They had definitely found each other.

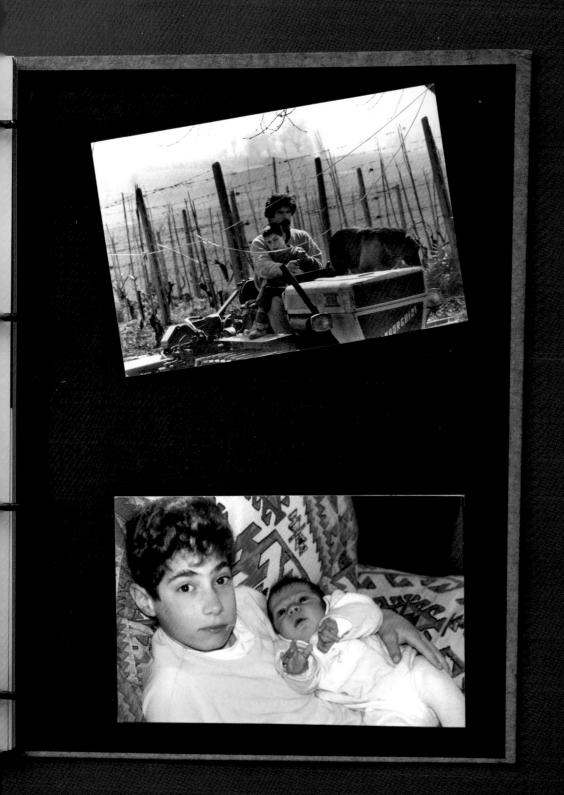

HIM WITH THE SHIRT

It's become a fight to dress you in the morning: you want to wear what you choose, without any trace of style. And many times you wear me down to such a point that I'm forced to send you to nursery school dressed in what I might call an indecent fashion. You are very stubborn. It's very difficult to get you to change your mind. You can't stand blackmail, you would rather go without; we can never say to you: 'If you do this, I'll give you that.' To us you are extraordinary.

From Rossella's diary, 1990

ROSSELLA On the day of Martina's confirmation, Marco was her godfather. He came down dressed in Adidas sweatpants, in that shiny material with three stripes – fuchsia, orange and I can't remember the other one – a black T-shirt with someone famous on it, maybe Jimi Hendrix, an Armani jacket, beautiful, and shoes, I think they were leopard skin ones. He was indecent and so I said: 'Marco, you're not coming like that are you?'

'No? Why not, don't I look good?' all proud.

'Go and change and at least put on a pair of jeans!'

I was happy with very little, I didn't ask for the moon. He went upstairs and after a while he came back down exactly as before but in his pants: shirt, jacket... and underpants. Then in the end he came dressed exactly as he'd wanted.

When it was his turn to be confirmed he wanted to wear a shirt that was nice but not suitable for confirmation. I can't remember if the trousers were jeans, and on top he had this orange shirt... at that time those tie-die shirts were all the rage. And I couldn't do anything; he wanted to go like that. When I went to collect the photos from the photographers I said: 'I'd like to collect the confirmation pictures.'

'Whose are they?'

'Simoncelli, Marco.'

'Oh god, who is he?' We're from Riccione and no-one knew us in Coriano. I described him a bit and then he worked it out: 'Ah, him with the shirt!' The shirt had made an impression!

I don't think Marco ever went into a shop to buy anything for himself. Sure, when he was a kid I'd buy what he needed. Then later there was always someone who'd dress him. But if he had to go round the shops himself he was totally useless. I remember one year, in Indianapolis, it was 2009 or 2010, Kate wasn't there because she was working and it was just us four. 'Come on, let's go for a look round the shops!' and off we went to Abercrombie. We wanted to buy something, me and Martina and, naturally, Marco didn't want to. He sat on a sofa and played with his phone, bored as hell to be there with us. 'Haven't you had enough yet?' he'd ask every so often.

I remember one great thing that often comes to mind: at 15, 16 years old Marco would go out cycling with a group of lads from round here. They'd meet at the Morciano–Migani fork and take off together: all these kids perfectly groomed from head to toe, all dressed like proper cyclists, with the lycra and so on... while he... well you had to see him, his get-up! He'd pull on his shabbiest fleecy tracksuit and be off. When I saw him I was so proud! Because I realised that he was himself and didn't need to portray himself in any other way: I am Marco, and that's that, whether I dress like this or like that is not important. He really had the courage to live, because he didn't have to appear or show himself to be like the others: he was himself, period.
   I admit though that sometimes he went over the top...

They send clothes to me
at home

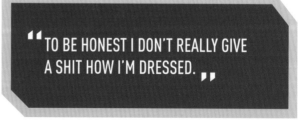

One thing we would always wind Marco up about, even if he later improved, was the way he dressed: he was like a German on holiday! Some of those flipflops... he really didn't give a shit about fashion! But one thing he should have done but didn't in the end was get dreadlocks. 'Just think, the first 'Rasta' of MotoGP!' I said to him. It would have been cool. But I think he was scared of Paolo, and he knew that then he'd have to cut it, his hair.

When we were small Dani and I wouldn't even stay in school until June, we would finish up early and spend a month and a half in Coriano with Marco, so there'd be months of mucking around. That year I'd just arrived in Coriano – I must have been twelve. Marco was nine, and said to me: 'Come on, let's go in that house, I've already been in there.'

We thought it was abandoned.

We went in through the door, there was maybe a 20-centimetre space, and once inside we went upstairs, we went all around, searching everywhere and then that joker picked up a broom handle and started to break the windows. 'Look at this!' Smash!

No problem, if it hadn't been for the fact that the owner showed up: he looked like the Monster of Florence! At that time the Monster was always on TV and in the papers. This guy was identical: vest, white hair, mean. He came in with a piece of wood with nails in it! We hid and I said: 'Marco, I'm not coming out.'

'Come out here!'

'I'm not coming out. We should jump down instead.'

'From the first floor? You're crazy, we'll break our legs!'

'I'm not coming out, we'll jump down here and run away.'

In the end we came out. We tried to run away but the guy grabbed us and whack! He hit one of us, then the other. He was shouting, spitting, we were terrified. 'Now go up there and close the windows! Who's going?' he said, and both of us: 'I'll go! I'll go.'

In the end I stayed put while Marco went up; he closed the windows and came back outside. The guy took us and put us in his car, both on the front seat next to him: me first, Marco on top, on my knees. Then he closed the door, went around and got in. Marco quickly opened the door and ran into the fields but, sitting under him, I didn't have time to get out before the guy was in front of the door. Marco was nice because when he saw that I was still in the car – he was already 20, 30 metres away, already in the field – he looked at me, came back and let the guy put him back in the car. He'd never leave a friend in his time of need.

The guy said: 'So where's home? I'm taking you, I'll make you...' 'That's our house there,' we told him. He started along the road, made another couple of turns and went straight on.

'No, our house was back there!'

'I don't care.'

'It was there! Where are we going?' And he said nothing.

We were very lucky that Coriano's carabinieri were not there, we got there and there was no-one! So he took us home. When they saw this crazy guy roll up, shouting at me and Marco who were as white as ghosts, our parents freaked out. My mum was there and Aunt Rossella. They calmed him down, apologised but they were a bit annoyed too of course.

That afternoon we found ourselves back at the carabinieri's station: Marco and me in one room, the guy in the other, they kept us separate. They got us to give our version of events, and he gave his. At a certain point one of the carabinieri came to us and said: 'He says you broke a window.'

'No no.'

So he left the room and we admitted to mum: 'It was us who broke the window.'

'Who was it?'

I didn't say anything, but they knew it was Marco.

When he came back again they told him: 'Look the boys say that they did break a window...'

And it went well because he told us: 'Ok, you've broken a window and it will cost 20,000 lire. That guy there can be done for kidnapping, hitting you... Let's close this here and now. The boys have had a shock and surely won't do it again.'

'No no no no!'

We did it again...

DANIELE	YOU HAVE TO FIND THE LIMIT

On the beach, at Valerio's beach club, everyone hated us because we were too rowdy. Valerio was an angel while his father couldn't stand us: we wanted to play bocce but he never wanted to give us the balls. So Marco would get mad. And the one time he did give them to us, and only because our parents asked, Marco made holes in the course.

There was also a children's slide on the beach. Fifty centimetres of slide! Marco would slide too slowly but we found that if you threw a bucket of water down while the other one was going down the slide then he'd go faster. The first time Marco did it sitting down. Then he wanted to go further: going down on his knees. The third time on his knees facing backwards. The fourth he had to do standing up.

MARCO IS LIKE THAT. HE EXPLAINED IT PERFECTLY. ONE TIME HE SAID: 'IT MIGHT SEEM LIKE BULLSHIT BUT THERE'S A PLAN: YOU HAVE TO FIND THE LIMIT.'

So anyway, Marco was on his feet, ready on the slide, a bucket of water... crash! He fell from the top and hit his head on the pavement. We were worried, we took him to A&E: he'd lost his memory and didn't remember a thing.

Even later on, when we were 13 or 14, whenever we went to the Aquafan water park it was the same. There was a slide where you had to wear a life jacket but Marco would pretend to lose his jacket as he came down, throwing it down and then following it. There were rapids too – with pools where you come down in a rubber ring, you stop, hit the other guys and then come down again – and Marco would throw his life jacket down at the first pool and then come down alone, bare-chested. Today that thing is all plastic, but at the time it was cement. Marco got to the bottom completely carved up. But he was happy because he'd done something he shouldn't have. And then there was another ride, Extreme, where you would come down in a rubber boat in pairs: the first time he went in front where it felt faster, the second time he went in front again, but facing backwards; the third time he complained to the lifeguard that he wanted to do it standing up.

'No, stop it, or I'll throw you out.'

'Come on, let me go down standing up, please.'

A disaster.

RICCARDO AND DANIELE   GRAND-PRIX RACING AT HOME

RICCARDO The first scooter that Marco had was a small 50cc that went like lightning. We'd made a little track using bamboo canes in the field in front of his house. At the time it was all very homemade: at first there was just the track, already made, and that red and white tape used during roadworks.

'Come on, let's try, let's try, get on.'

I got on the scooter, I don't even know if it had gears, and at a certain point I didn't know what was going on any more – I was going straight with the tape stretched to the limit and me and the bike were about to go into the house, I didn't know how to stop. But Marco was already fast. We would make races around the house, we would time the laps, all very professional. At that time the lap involved passing in front of the house, going down the hill, then you'd get to the reference point – we'd put a brick or something – you'd go around it and back up. We'd take turns and then it was Dani's go...

DANIELE And I said to him: 'Now I'll show you!' Helmet on with the visor up... I went down the hill and at a certain point one of the bamboo canes that was sticking out into the road hit me right in the face, whack! Like a whip. I lost control, badly scraped. I had been sandpapered, there was blood everywhere.

RICCARDO So much time passed, Marco and I asked each other what could have happened. Then Dani came up the hill, limping. We looked at each other... 'And the bike?!'

DANIELE They didn't give a shit as to whether I'd hurt myself!

RICCARDO We also got up to all sorts in the fields. When we were very small there was this little house where we'd play by the river. It was on the bank and we'd play at jumping the ditch. We'd often get hurt there, and badly. We would climb trees, run, jump, play at crossing the river and falling in... Marco would break the branch on purpose. The last time we did it I was 25 years old, it was New Year and the water on 31 December wasn't exactly warm...

DANIELE Also at the foundry, at granny's, there was a really cool play area. In the middle of the garden there were stacks of containers where they would dispose of the aluminium scraps. On the bicycle, granny's legendary Graziella that had seen all sorts of ramps and jumps, we had to quickly jump up. One time, as I jumped, my shirt got caught on the iron staircase that you used to go up and I ripped my chest open. I still have the scar. Other times we'd take two bricks and a piece of wood and we'd make a ramp. Granny was really happy...

> **"** MY FIRST TIME WAS A REALLY EMOTIONAL EXPERIENCE FOR ME, FOR HER A BIT LESS MAYBE... SHE WAS OLDER, EXPERIENCED, BY THAT I MEAN SHE WAS THE VILLAGE BICYCLE, EVERYONE HAD HAD A RIDE. **"**

When you see a person as a rival you can't see the positives. The more people spoke well of Marco to me, the less I understood what they meant. I found him strange, and I found his family a little strange too. Now, on the other hand, I admit that that family is to be admired. They are wonderful people and the only family present at every race, whether in Italy or around the world. A real family like those in the movies, which clashes a little with our world. In the paddock this kind of thing doesn't usually exist.

BUT THAT IS A FAMILY THAT HAS ALWAYS WANTED TO LIVE AS A REAL FAMILY: THE DAD IS THE DAD, THE MUM IS THE MUM, THE SON IS THE SON, DESPITE BEING A RIDER, THE DAUGHTER IS THE DAUGHTER, AND THE GIRLFRIEND IS THE GIRLFRIEND. AND IT'S BEAUTIFUL, ESPECIALLY IN TODAY'S GP CHAMPIONSHIP, TO SEE A THING LIKE THAT; LIKE SOMETHING FROM ANOTHER ERA.

People with a common goal, with the aim to win the championship together. It's very difficult to have a good father–son relationship and I have always viewed the relationship between Marco and Paolo as an unusual one. Perhaps too unusual...

WHEN WE WERE RACING MINIBIKES I USED TO TAKE THE PISS BECAUSE MARCO WAS ONE OF VERY FEW, PERHAPS THE ONLY ONE, TO GO AROUND HOLDING HIS DAD'S HAND. 'IT'S UNREAL, LOOK AT THAT DORK,' I USED TO THINK.

But no, it's not right or wrong, it depends on the character of both the parents and the children. If I imagine myself, hand in hand with my dad... I can't even think about it, crazy! But with Marco's character, with his dad's character, it was right for them. For them it was the best way to share things, to transfer values from father to son.

I am a father too, but I am a bit scared: bringing up children with the right values is difficult in today's world, it's very complicated, and I'd like to know how it's done because this, as a parent, is particularly important.

I THINK ALMOST EVERYONE IN THE WORLD WOULD HAVE LIKED TO HAVE BEEN SIMONCELLI, TO HAVE LIVED LIKE HIM, DESPITE HIS DEATH AT 24 YEARS OLD. BECAUSE HE LIVED 24 WONDERFUL YEARS, WITH A WONDERFUL FAMILY THAT ALWAYS HELPED HIM TO FOLLOW HIS DREAM. ONE OF THE GREAT THINGS ABOUT MARCO IS THAT EVERYTHING HE DID, HE DID IN A BLAZE, AT FULL SPEED. THEY CAN'T HAVE ANY REGRETS. NOT HIM, NOT HIS FAMILY.

If I think about my career on the other hand I do have regrets: I often played it safe, I held myself back, always looking to the future. Sure, I can say that this paid off in the end.

Basically there is no one foolproof method that suits everyone, but if I look at Marco, even if I never agreed with what he did, I think he did well, that he shouldn't have done anything differently. Because if he had held back during those years, it would have been worse. Maybe...

VALENTINO ROSSI	A FAMILY LIKE THOSE IN THE MOVIES

Sic had an amazing relationship with his dad, very rare I think for a 24-year-old guy. We were very different in this respect, because I have a great relationship with my dad but sometimes I prefer to be with my friends, I think that's normal.

BUT IN HIS CASE, SHIT, MAYBE HIS FATHER WAS HIS BEST FRIEND.

This is a special thing. Because usually you get close to your dad again after a few years but when you're 20 you just want to do your own thing.

3. BIG WHEELS

GIUGNO 2000 - LE PR

CEROTTO
I CADUTA 125 (MAGIONE)

PLASTER, 1ST CRASH IN 125 (MAGIONE)

PROVE ooo CHE BRIVIDO ooo

JUNE 2000 – THE FIRST TESTS... WHAT A THRILL!!!

3. BIG WHEELS

GIUGNO 2000 - LE PR

CEROTTO
I CADUTA 125 (MAGIONE)

PLASTER, 1ST CRASH IN 125 (MAGIONE)

PROVE... CHE BRIVIDO !!!

JUNE 2000 – THE FIRST TESTS... WHAT A THRILL!!!

> **"I COULD SEE THAT EVERYTHING WAS COMING EASILY TO ME AND I SAID, LORD, COME ON, LET'S GIVE IT A TRY."**

THE BIG LEAP

PAOLO In 2001 we decided to make the big leap and move up to the big wheels. The biggest problem was that we needed to find money.

The first thing to do is find the bike: you go to a guy that races, we went to Fausto Ricci, and you say: 'I have a kid who wants to try it, how much do you want?' Then if he's capable, if he likes it, you have to find a team. Maybe you go back to the guy who let you try the bike and you say: 'How much for you to put us in the Italian championship?' and he'll tell you 50, 70, 80,000 euro... You decide where you want to go, you make a contract, you pay the agreed amount and they give you the structure, mechanic and bike ready to race. It's a business.

Then, if you ride well, you must try to get to the World Championship. The system there is the same; it's just that the numbers are much higher. If you want to run in the World series you have to find 200, 300,000 euro. The costs are exorbitant for teams too, not so much for the bike but for the travel costs. This system makes me mad – the rider is exploited, when at the end of the day he is the one keeping the show alive.

Across the entire World Championship very few riders make money, there's real passion and then, inevitably, the faster you go the more conditions improve. In 2004, when they told us that they liked Marco as a rider and didn't want any payment, it was like winning the lottery, though the first real money came later, in 2006–7 with Aprilia.

So the problem of money was immediately pressing: we needed cash to do the Honda trophy, the Italian championship, a few races in the European championship. I started to pay visits to companies and my advantage was that I had a boy who was winning, who was fast and likeable. For this reason I usually took Marco along with me: on the one side he needed to understand what we were doing and on the other I had realised that people were more willing when they had this kid in front of them; you could see the hunger to race in his eyes.

A certain man called Anselmo ran a bar in Ospedaletto di Coriano and all day long he'd be inundated with folk who'd go there for breakfast, for an aperitivo... I took him ice-cream, he had taken to Marco and would hassle all his clients, telling them that the boy needed help because he was fast. At one point he took the guys from Pascucci coffee aside and told them: 'Listen, if you want me to continue using your coffee you need to give this kid money.' Practically blackmail. So, in order not to lose his client, the area manager spoke to his bosses and they arranged a meeting with us at the Pascucci shop in Rimini. We went in, they looked at us, and then this brawny guy got up and offered us a tiny amount, a few euro.
   At that point Marco said: 'Nooo, why?' Mario Pascucci also got up, saw the boy, looked at him and asked: 'But how much do you need?' Marco blurted out a high figure and he said: 'OK, I'll give it to you'. Pascucci had been won over. He was one of the fundamental people during those initial years: he allowed us to get started and helped us a lot at the start, and the Pascucci coffee brand remained for good. One year Mario had invested heavily to build a new warehouse and was in trouble but Marco always wore his brand regardless.

Another person that gave us a hand early on and really helped us break into the circle was Roberto Marchionni, who as well as designing the helmets also introduced us to Matteoni and helped us find money. Later the relationship with him got more complicated because as Marco grew up we decided to go to Drudi, so we each went our separate ways.

SPEAKING OF SPONSORS

ROSSELLA Speaking of sponsors, Marco took part in an episode of *Scherzi a parte* ('Joking Aside') in 2009. For starters, I thought that the victim would know about the joke ahead of time but he actually didn't know anything at all.

That morning Marco was having breakfast when the 'police' arrived. It was great because he carried on eating his breakfast, with his back to them as they came in. At a certain point the policeman said: 'Look, you have to come with us because we have a video of you taking part in illegal street racing, there's money involved...'

Marco almost laughed and the serious guy said: 'Look, it's not a laughing matter, please go and get dressed so we can leave.'

The evening before, Paolo and I, in on the joke, were thinking: 'OK, so tomorrow morning these guys are going to show up and take him away, it would be better if he had some Rifle clothing to hand.' Marco was sponsored by Rifle, a company founded in '58... So I had put everything else away, leaving his Rifle clothes at the front so he'd find them easily. He went upstairs – I followed him and said, desperately: 'But what have you done Marco?' and he replied: 'Mum, try and pretend to be calm' – and when he came back down I think he had on a yellow shirt with a ghost on it. 'Where the hell did he go and get that shirt from?' I was thinking, but of course I couldn't say anything.

Anyway, he left and we followed him in our car because they didn't want us with them of course. When he got out of the fake vehicle he even apologised for having laughed back home: 'Look I laughed before because I couldn't hold it in. I go drifting yes but I don't make illegal bets. I know nothing about that... that's why I wanted to laugh.' We were in the room behind and from there we could see everything that was happening on the monitors.

Afterwards I asked him: 'Marco but why did you choose that shirt, I had put out...' And can you believe it, Marco, shocked although he knew he hadn't done anything wrong, told me: 'Maybe I don't exactly drive by the book, it's true, but I definitely don't take part in illegal races. So I knew I hadn't done anything wrong, but what if there were pictures... I go on TV, they see me with a Rifle shirt, what a bad impression would I make for the sponsors?'

Who would have thought of that? Marco had enormous respect for others.

TEN SECONDS SIMONCELLI!

PAOLO Massimo Matteoni had a fundamental role in Marco's career and they had a wonderful relationship. He is a man of great charisma; Marco adored him and hung off his every word, he didn't miss a trick; everything that Matteoni said was committed to memory.

With him, we started off doing the Honda trophy. As he was doing the World Championship, he couldn't come with us and sent us to races with a mechanic, a good guy, but he was doing it as a second job. I think Massimo realised later that he'd made a mistake with Marco, at the start. I remember that, at that time, he was crashing a lot, four, five times per race, and we couldn't understand why. I watched him from the side of the track and he seemed to be riding well. Finally we realised that, because he'd moved directly to the 125 class, Marco had continued to ride as he did on the minibike, where you had to keep your feet at almost ninety degrees.

After the Honda trophy we went to Spain to take part in the last two races of the Spanish championship as it meant good visibility. Matteoni had told him: 'Come on, let's go and do these two races.' 'Come on, get your money out,' he told me. In the first race at Valencia Marco did great, he finished fifth. All his future GP rivals were there, he crossed the line with the frontrunners and it was fantastic. So we headed on to Jerez. After the Valencia race he was so pumped up and Matteoni continued to tell him: 'Look, at Jerez, with those long turns at the back of the track, they'll have ten seconds on you, ten seconds Simoncelli!' Marco went out on track, made a few laps and at a certain point saw Giansanti in front of him. 'Right, dammit, now I'm going to pass you and take the lap record,' he thought. But instead he crashed! It was there that he realised he needed to stay calm, but that was his nature: 'I go in and take the record. If I went well at Valencia, here I'll take the record.'

At Jerez we risked not qualifying because up until three minutes before the end of practice he was lapping really slowly. Then he came across Lai, who already had a couple of years of experience, he stuck with him and just managed to qualify. I think he was eighteenth. The evening before the race he took Matteoni's scooter to an MX track that was close to the circuit and crashed, wrecking the scooter. He rang me: 'Dad, come here. Dad, come here. I fell with the scooter, how are we going to tell Matteoni?!' Later I told him: 'Massimo, have you seen what Marco did?' And he said: 'It doesn't matter, I don't care!' Massimo was like that. When I complimented Marco Massimo would say: 'Naa, it's not true.' Other times he would defend Marco

– I said: 'He fell with the scooter', I was angry but he just said: 'Naa, it's OK.' Matteoni was good with the kids, he'd been a rider himself so he knew when to encourage them and when to be tough.

One time we were testing at Almeria. It was raining but Marco wanted to ride anyway of course, and he didn't just want to go round and round. He insisted that a mechanic stayed at the pit-wall with the board to give him his times, because he wanted to know how he was doing in order to improve. So in the pouring rain this poor guy had to give him his times at the end of each lap. I was watching Marco from the terrace and could see that at the end of the straight he was braking later with each lap. And I knew that sooner or later he wouldn't make the turn… He completes five, six, ten laps… Then at one point he brakes, hard. Bam! Crash! He loses the front, and slides past the front of the pits.

At dinner we used to talk about the day and that evening I said to Massimo: 'Bloody hell, another crash!' and he said: 'No problem, keep braking later Simoncelli, keep braking later!' He was encouraging him to try and brake later each time, I would shout at Marco while he would let him off!

Marco adored Massimo, he adored him for his jokes, for his stories, he was like his master. Marco would absorb everything, when you told him things he would always listen, and Massimo was his teacher when it came to both riding and life. When he talked about Matteoni, Marco would get animated, he had fun, he'd imitate him all the time and would remember even the smallest things, I don't know how he did it. Even in later years he'd come out with a Matteoni joke or turn of phrase every so often. He cared a lot for him, even if he treated us badly at times.

One day at Most he gave him a good telling off that wasn't very nice, and the kid started to cry. Massimo went off to eat in the hospitality unit, at a table outside, and after a while, having seen that Marco was crying, he said: 'Come here Simoncelli', and there at the table he calmly told him what he should have done.

Matteoni was great. And Marco would stockpile everything he learned, he wouldn't discard anything. So that week I took him to the square and made chicanes with rubbish bins, because it looked like his biggest problem was that he didn't move on the bike, not leaning over at all.

LET'S GO AND MAKE A LAP

PAOLO In 2002 we started to take part in a few World Championship races, Brno and the five after that. In the meantime we'd won the European championship and so we couldn't go to Japan because we had the final European race, at Cartagena. Marco rode really well and won: he'd won the European championship so at the end of the race he started doing burnouts, making the tyres smoke, so much so that the bike stopped running. The piston had seized and Massimo had also given him a really extreme bike. So we were waiting, waiting but Marco didn't arrive... In the end he came along on one of the track's emergency vehicles!

That evening we celebrated; Matteoni had a truck with a lounge area inside, Castagna was there preparing food. We went there to celebrate, drank a bit and then loaded our bags into the car because we needed to catch a plane in Valencia. We had an Opel Corsa that was full to bursting and during the celebrations Marco kept saying to Matteoni: 'Massimo, come on, let's go and make a lap of the track', and he: 'Naa, Simoncelli, naa.' Massimo is right when he says that Marco never gave him a moment's peace. When he wanted something he was insistent, it was crazy. So we headed out to leave for the airport and Matteoni said: 'Come on Simoncelli, let's go and make a lap', and I said: 'Shit, no, but no...'

They had this running challenge. It had all started when they were racing the rental cars at a karting track, in Braga. Marco would stitch him up every time and Matteoni couldn't take it! One race after another, always level with each other, until the carabinieri showed up and turned off the track's lights, forcing them to stop. Matteoni said to Marco: 'If we win the European title we'll finish this.' One week later we had the race at Cartagena and, no sooner said than done, he kept his promise.

On the first lap Matteoni drove and the car was touching the ground with the weight of all the luggage! On the second lap he stopped and Marco took over. At a certain point I saw a lot of smoke through the fast turn in front of the pits.

'Have they rolled?'

And Malabrocca said: 'No, they haven't rolled.'

But they had rolled. Twice.

The circuit director was so angry, he called the police so Matteoni planned to tell them that he was driving as he had a licence! Marco was only 15 at the time. The police said that anyone could drive there, as it was a track, but the director wasn't happy, he wanted to report them and so they took them away and kept them at the station until midnight. Until I, accompanied by a Spanish kid who would translate, went to explain to the police chief that Marco had won the European championship and that he'd be racing in the World Championship the following week, and so he was happy, had been celebrating and had made a mistake. They understood and sent us away after getting me to sign a paper stating that I would pay for any damage to the track.

We had to fly four hours later, we were car-less and so it was lucky that my cousin Roberto had travelled from Riccione to watch that race. I rang him, he came to get us, took us to Valencia and that was that.

The best bit of the story was that Marco had a contract with Dainese, they provided him with his leathers and helmets and had told him: 'Look, this year we can only give you the material but if you win the European championship we'll add 10 million lire.' Great, we put the 10 million towards the 20 million owed for damage to the car, they paid half each: 10 from Marco, 10 from Matteoni.

YOU'VE GOT THE KNACK!

Not long ago you started driving the car, or rather cars, because you've tried all of them: my Tipo, the Mercedes, granny's car, Aunt Lola's car, the Fiorino and I must say that you've got the knack!

From Rossella's diary, 2001

ROSSELLA Marco was 14, 15. In the afternoon I would be at the ice-cream parlour and my mother would be at home with him. Granddad Mario, my father-in-law, had just changed his car and had left his old Panda at our place. Marco had the keys to that Panda and the things he'd get up to! In the neighbouring field they'd cut the corn and so it was an open space and he'd drive up and down like a crazy thing. The field was on a hill, it was getting dangerous. My mother called for him, shouted at him... she was desperate. She told him not to do it but Marco didn't listen. So she called me at the parlour and said: 'What should I do with your son?! He's here with that car, I've had enough!' Every day was the same, with the issue of the car, until we took the keys away! And we did the same with the Brutale that they'd got for him when he won his first 250 race. When we saw this bike arriving at the house – it was a beautiful bike – we got scared, and so we put it away with a chain and padlock on it!

AH.... AN SAVEM

I remember when Marco used to come to my workshop each day to adjust his bicycle or scooter; he'd spend whole days there working with us.

I started by letting Marco race with a little Honda in the Italian championship and Honda trophy, that year we went to do our first test in Hungary and I remember that I was angrier than I'd ever been in my life... He was messing everything up, he came from the world of minibikes and knew absolutely nothing about race bikes!

HE WAS STUBBORN BUT HAD A BIG HEART.

During the return trip in the car with his dad I was able to make him understand where he was going wrong and how he should use the bike. It was no easy task but our journey started from there.

In the next race he reached the podium and that brought great satisfaction for everybody. This experience taught Marco to listen to my advice and, above all, to his dad Paolo's advice. From then on we continued to grow, in terms of both spirit and character. And Marco sure had character.

We did everything we could to ensure that the Italian championship and Honda trophy went as well as possible and we came out winners.

Enormous sacrifices were made, especially by Paolo, in order to be able to buy an Aprilia RS with which to compete in the European championship the following year but all of the sacrifices paid off, as Marco completed a unique season. To achieve this result, me and his trusted mechanic, Sanzio Raffaelli, missed the Motegi Grand Prix in order to be with Marco at the last European race and make him champion. The title didn't come without controversy: we were accused of having used special parts. If you think about it it's true, we did have a special part... Marco!

That same year Marco became part of my World team, as a substitute rider, from the Brno round until the end of the championship.

The following year, with the help of Mario Pascucci, Marco took part in his first complete World Championship; he didn't do badly, considering too the small budget available. His best result was fourth at Valencia.

I don't have anything to add about his career, the rest is now a part of history, and I don't have the words to describe a guy that was so honest with me as well as all of those around him.

Marco wasn't any old rider, he was an honest rider, he had heart. His father and I taught him the values of life and he, during his brief journey on this earth, passed these on.

Ciao Marco. Together we did so many crazy things and you will always be number one in my heart, as a rider but above all as an honest and spontaneous guy.

I'll see you soon. Ciao Marco!

> **" I DID ENOUGH DAMAGE AT 14, I WAS ALWAYS BUSTED UP, SKIN PEELING OFF, EITHER WITH MY BICYCLE OR MY SCOOTER. I COULD NEVER DO ANYTHING RIGHT. "**

SANZIO RAFFAELLI (MALABROCCA) | **YOU TWO ARE CRAZY**

At 18, when Marco got his licence, he came to my house that evening and rang the doorbell, totally unexpected. He wanted to go drifting with his father's Mercedes in the car parks and I, being older, tried to discourage him. But it was impossible. So we went to the car parks in Riccione, him at the wheel and me next to him. Once inside, he'd point the wheel at the centre of the turn, then full throttle, handbrake and an unbelievable screeching of tyres. People rolled down their windows and shouted: 'You two are crazy, we'll call the carabinieri!' until we left. And, once, the police really did show up...

When he was racing with team Matteoni, Marco would wait for me at the roundabout by the autostrada in Riccione and we'd see who would arrive at the racing department first: him on his scooter or me, an old crazy, in my Opel Corsa. We could have lost our licences, the things we did! It was a great battle: my car gave me the advantage but Marco was convinced he'd beat me because he was on two wheels.

TO BE MARCO'S FRIEND YOU CAN'T BE COMPLETELY NORMAL: WE'RE ALL A LITTLE 'FULL THROTTLE'!

When Paolo and Marco showed up at Matteoni's racing department with that Honda enduro bike, ready to go to the Cava, both Matteoni and I thought: 'You're probably going to go and hurt yourself on that thing.' Marco then decided to buy the Yamaha that Valentino Rossi had used the year before and with that bike he started a whole series of tests... I taught him the ABC of off-roading, and he was so good on this Yamaha, that wasn't great from a mechanical point of view, that he started battling with Valentino at the Cava. Out of this a great 'friendly rivalry' was born and... well, at the Cava they got up to all sorts.

PAOLO   In minibikes Marco started racing with number 7, Eddie Lawson's number. He also had Eddie Lawson's helmet, an old helmet of mine that had saved my life in a serious accident. Even though it was big on him and moved around on his head, I was pleased to give it to him and he wore it for quite a while, in his first races. When Lawson came to see him at Laguna Seca last year I remember that Marco told him that he was his idol when he was young, and that he'd raced with his helmet and his number... But with the minibikes the numbers changed all the time because they used the number you finished with. Marco rode with 5, with 2, with 1 and once, at Castelraimondo, even with 13...

Number 58 was an accident, the fact that his mum was born in '58 had nothing to do with it. For the European 125 championship we had chosen 55, but it was already taken by another rider, and so we got stuck with 58.

But then he won the European championship with 58 and so from then on it was his official number and we never changed it, Marco continued to get stronger and his connection with his number became stronger still.

THESE EXTRAORDINARY THIRTEEN YEARS

I find it difficult to describe Marco during this time of transformation; it would have been easier a while ago... I consider him mature for his age anyway – it's probably his interest in anything and everything, and not only school-related things, that makes him pretty self-assured in different situations.

He's very curious and though on the one hand I think this is a great thing that pushes him to learn new things, sometimes his slightly intrusive behaviour can become irritating... I hope that as he grows up he is able to strike a balance.

He hides a very delicate sensitivity that almost takes me by surprise sometimes. He also worries, not just about things that concern him but also about those around him. He strongly believes in the things he does and is almost always certain that he'll succeed. He loves to be rewarded. He's very competitive and this side of Marco is great on the one hand because it pushes him to do his best, but on the other hand...

He's reflective, even if it might look as if he's not absorbing what you're saying. In recent years he has had a wonderful relationship with his father, also because they spend so much time together and have so much to share. The sport that Marco practises has undoubtedly contributed to this symbiosis. He has perhaps grown a little further apart from me for different reasons: his age, the arrival of his sister who takes up my time which was once all his...

Anyone who has had the chance to spend time with Marco will have surely noticed the lack of urgency, the lack of speed with which he deals with his things, regardless of the interest he might have; it almost seems that time has no meaning for him, that it doesn't pass... there's always time for everything... having to respect schedules is really exasperating for him.
This too is part of his personality, a quality that is in stark contrast to the competitive sport that he practises, in which one hundredth of a second can make all the difference. For those who are close to him in his day to day life it's surprising and almost unbelievable to see the transformation once he gets on the bike: speed, concentration, tenacity and determination become normal things for him.

Marco has many dreams for the future, and this too is normal for his age... it would be sad if the opposite were true. These extraordinary thirteen years are like that: so beautiful in different ways... seeing this growth that is both so fast and so tremendously slow at the same time... every day is a battle and you need to know how to measure everything out to obtain a positive result, which I think is every parent's objective.

Based on Marco's profile for middle school, compiled by Rossella in January 2000

UNGIORNO DIVENTERO'

WORLD CHAMPION

THE BIRTH CHART

ROSSELLA Marco was an extremely sensitive boy. This is why, when his primary school teacher called me to tell me that Marco had hit a boy in the bathroom, I was so upset about it. You see your son in a certain way, and then of course you're disappointed when you hear that he does certain things.

Coming home I asked him what had happened and he told me that he had hit the boy because as he was going into the bathroom he had seen that boy hit another smaller child, so he had intervened to defend him... So he wasn't exactly in the wrong.

When Marco was three and a half, a girl had done a birth chart for him but I didn't recognise him in it at all. But over the years, reading it over again, I realised just how spot on it was. It said that when he grew up he could become a pilot or dedicate himself to some kind of humanitarian work: doing something for others basically.

WHY?

'Mummy, did you know that grandpa Italo helped me with my science homework today? It was so difficult and I was worried I'd get it wrong. So I asked grandpa to help me and it went well after that. I got an A, and it was an important grade. I'm sure that it was grandpa, I could feel him there next to me, and when I looked up to thank him, mummy, I saw him reflected in the sky.'

From Rossella's diary, 1993

ROSSELLA Emilia, Marco's primary school teacher, told me that when he arrived at school he wouldn't have his backpack on his shoulder like everyone else: he'd take it off, put it on the top step and then bump bump bump. He'd kick it and it would take the stairs, as he put it. She would of course hear him even before he arrived in the classroom and she'd get so angry: she was very strict, Emilia.

She also told me that Marco had his desk up against the teacher's desk and when they were given work to do, he would make a mountain of books and exercise books. He would ask his classmates to lend him their books, to make a barrier. And then he'd stoop down to hide. He'd get into so much trouble, also because he was always bent over... She told him that if carried on like that he'd turn into the Hunchback of Notre Dame. Then when the kids were outside playing football they'd always end up fighting of course. So she would come along and say: 'I'll be referee!' And Marco: 'Miss, but what does a referee who knows nothing about football do?!'

Another teacher, Giovanna, always told me that in 30 years of teaching, she'd never known anyone who as was as much of a pain in the butt as Marco. Perhaps she was explaining something in class – she taught history – and Marco would keep saying 'Why?' And then he'd answer back, she would answer him and he'd say: 'Yes, but...' and in the end she'd get embarrassed, she didn't know what to say and would shout at him: 'That's enough Marco, stop it, let me continue.' Even at home he would wear me out during the 'Why?' years.

In middle school, I can't remember if he was in the second or third year, he came home one day saying: 'Mum! Borgese – his technical drawing teacher – slapped me!' In that moment I was taken aback but said to him: 'Marco, what did you do? If he did that to you, you must have deserved it!' And he said: 'Wait, you don't care? You don't understand, he slapped me!' He nagged me about it all afternoon. He was useless at technical drawing, but he also took advantage: he'd never take his ruler, square ruler, papers, nothing. The teacher was undoubtedly ticked off that day and clouted him. It happens. He hadn't exactly come home with a black eye! But he was surprised by my reaction and kept on saying: 'You think he was right to slap me?!'

At school, you and some others had teased or played a joke on a classmate. The teacher was very angry and asked those responsible to raise their hands. You and Mattia were the only ones brave and honest enough to admit to it. I praised you for doing that, it was the right thing to do and the fact that you told me you thought of grandpa when the teacher asked you the question is significant. These last two days you've brought us coffee in bed.

From Rossella's diary, 1993

ROSSELLA Marco often brought us coffee in bed. I went to bed very late, at 3 or 4am because we had the ice-cream parlour and he'd come and bring me coffee at 8 in the morning... I'm telling you, if there's one thing I hate it's coffee on an empty stomach, I really can't drink it! But, poor kid, he'd come up with a tray... how could I say: 'No, I don't want it'? If he stayed put I had to choke it down, that coffee. If I was lucky and he went straight back downstairs I would throw it down the sink. Now it's him who comes to me and says: 'Mum! Mum! Get me a coffee?'

MISSING CREDIT

ROSSELLA Marco didn't like things to be simple. He liked to fight, he liked to struggle to obtain things, to sweat, no short-cuts. Right from when he was small. When he would do his homework I would keep an eye on him, maybe he would make a mistake and I'd say: 'Hang on Marco, that's wrong there, it's not like that.' But he wouldn't listen. He'd take the homework to school as he had done it and would get the teacher to correct it. He'd made a mistake, but he wasn't scared for people to see that.

But once, at high school, he behaved in the totally opposite way to normal. He was a credit short, in technical drawing obviously, and after four years he still hadn't made it up. So he had to do this project in class that involved a drawing. He went to school, the teacher gave him a drawing to do but he couldn't do it. Two hours later and the page was still blank. She gave him another chance: 'Ok, we'll do it next week.' He came home, put the figures together and got a friend to do the drawing for him, with the idea that: 'Next time, I'll give this in as my work.'
 The following week rolled around, he went back to school and the teacher wanted to give him a different drawing to do of course. He persuaded her to give him the same one as before and she agreed. But from that moment on she hovered over him the whole time, not leaving him for a second, like a guard. Marco's friends called her to try and distract her but she stayed with him.
 At the end of the two hours, he hadn't done anything. At a certain point the teacher got distracted for a second and Marco was finally able to swap the pages. She turned around, saw the drawing... She was so mad; she started looking for the blank page but couldn't find it.

When Marco came home, he told me everything and I told him he was an idiot. 'God dammit,' I said. He didn't make up the credit. His teacher called me to tell me what had happened, she was very angry. I of course apologised while Marco wanted me to go and tell her that the drawing was his! He was spirited.
 The problem was solved the following year when he changed school because when you change school any missing credits are absolved. Marco should have started the fifth year but in the meantime he'd changed category, moving up to 250. There were more test sessions, more commitments with his work and we thought he wouldn't be able to cope with high school. But he had to finish, having completed four years he couldn't give up. I always pushed for school as, apart from the importance of having the diploma, I wanted Marco

to have a normal life, like his classmates, so he had to go to lessons, do his homework, sit the tests...

He always said that he only went to school to keep me happy, but in the end he was happy too. We thought that the best way to deal with that fifth year was for him to study privately before taking the exam at the end. He wanted to do it there, at the Volta school where he'd always gone, but it wasn't possible, so he got a diploma in community management which would at least allow him to go on to university if he chose to do so one day. So that May he had to sit exams in all the subjects he didn't know, like psychology... even home economics, they had actually taught him to sew on buttons! I would burst out laughing when he would practise with those buttons!

AT THE ICE-CREAM PARLOUR

ROSSELLA It was the summer of 2001 and Marco had decided to work at the parlour to help out and earn some money. He would take his bicycle and in that heat he would come down from Coriano to Riccione where he needed to arrive by midday to get ready for opening: wipe the surfaces down, clean the glass, get the different ice-creams out of the freezers and put them on the counters, turn the lights on... But he was always late, there was no way to get him there for midday. That first year, seeing as he'd caused an accident, wrecking his dad's scooter by running into his uncle's Opel Corsa, he didn't collect any wages at all, that way he repaid the damage he'd caused. That year went like that, and so the following year he'd take his wages every evening, to be sure... He would say: 'Today I did three, four hours' and he'd pocket the amount that we'd agreed on.

Every so often when he left the parlour he would stop and help the street vendor that had a stand out front, he'd become his friend. But a turning point came when a local photographer offered him some work at his shop. I was pleased because I hoped that this new job would force him to be a bit more punctual, more meticulous. But instead he could go whenever he wanted, with no fixed hours. The photographer would go to Misano to shoot the guys on the track, even if they were just lapping for fun; he didn't know the difference and Marco's job was to divide the photos according to bike type. He was great at that.

SKIVING

Your only flaw is your slowness, your inability to get your daily tasks done quickly and efficiently. But if you didn't have this defect you'd be too perfect. I love you so much.

From Rossella's diary, 2004

> **"** VALENTINO HAS A DEFECT IN THAT HE ALWAYS SHOWS UP LATE... BUT SO DO I. **"**

ROSSELLA Arriving late was precisely his goal. He'd start doing stupid, pointless things just to show up late. It was great when he arranged to meet Valentino, maybe they'd call each other: 'So where are you?' 'I'm going to be an hour later than late!'

Of course Marco would also turn up late for school, especially when he started going alone on his scooter. The first time the teacher said, 'OK', the second time, 'OK', the third time he shut the door in his face: 'You're not coming in, go to the headteacher.' He would go and the head would send him back to class.

In 2005 he was in the fourth year of high school and it was the start of January, it was nearly the 20th and he would turn 18. One day he said to me: 'So, mum, before the 20th I have to skive off school just once!'

Because he'd never done it, he was mature enough to understand that, with all the absences he already had, he couldn't miss school when he was home. While once he was 18, he could make his own decisions and there'd be no fun in it anymore.

"I GREW UP WITH THE LEGEND THAT WAS VILLENEUVE: MY DAD PASSED IT ON TO ME. I WAS ALSO A FAN OF HIS SON, IN FACT I WENT AGAINST THE TIDE, BECAUSE AT THAT TIME EVERYONE ELSE IN ITALY SUPPORTED SCHUMACHER."

VILLENEUVE

Your father really pushes down hard on the accelerator while you take the wheel, sitting on his knee, and I must say that you know what you're doing.
You're not yet eight years old.
You often watch the tape of Gilles Villeneuve.

From Rossella's diary, 1995

ROSSELLA At 13, 14 years old, Marco could watch that video about Gilles Villeneuve's career, that finished with his death, ten times a day. And now, thinking about it, I say: 'Look at that, he died in the same way, his helmet flying off.' And we could say that Marco was as generous as Gilles. They had many things in common. It was probably that that scared me, at the time. The Villeneuve thing really bothered me. It bothered Paolo too, he said: 'That's enough. I'm taking the video away! I don't want you watching it, I'd rather you watched porn!'

PAOLO When certain things happen you sure can't help but wonder. I wasn't fanatical about him but Villeneuve had made a certain impression on me, for his riding style and above all for the fact that he never gave up. Villeneuve taught me this and I tried to teach Marco the same thing, he would watch those Villeneuve tapes and he liked them because I had told him the man's story.

As well as the videos, I had bought a rose that they had named after Villeneuve, and I planted it in the garden of our house in Riccione. This rose had wonderful flowers, a deep red velvet, incredibly beautiful. When we moved to Coriano in '88 I uprooted it and replanted it, and the rose continued to flower every year. But then it died the summer that Marco died. A coincidence that moved me.

The other day we received a painting from someone who had depicted Villeneuve in the car and Marco behind, on the bike... I think that people my age saw the connection between their racing styles and the fact they were both so strong. But as individuals they must have been quite different. Marco loved people, he liked to be hugged, to sign autographs... I remember that each time we went to an event he would say: 'Dad, did you hear the applause? The loudest applause was for me!' He cared a lot about his fans, he never said no to anyone. But they say that Villeneuve was a bit of a snob, he was one of those that'd travel around in his helicopter... but in the car he would do just what Marco did on his bike.

At school Marco was straightforward, level-headed, pragmatic, a boy of few words. His essays were also short, but rich in content. The best thing is that he was loyal, he would keep a pact and stick to his word. He was a good listener, there was no need to repeat things to him three times and this made me think of him as a man, even though he was a boy. He would always find himself facing up to challenges that were bigger than him and he had grown as a result. For years I kept a sheet of paper, a sheet of stickers that his mum had brought me at the start of the year. It was the GP calendar, so that I'd know when Marco would be in class.

| MATTIA TOMBESI | IN COMPETITION |

At primary school they gave us a project, 'Describe your best friend', so Marco described me and I described him. We practically grew up together and have been friends forever, going through primary, middle and four years of high school together. We'd see each other in the afternoons when we'd play football, I'd go to his house or he'd come to mine and we did all those things that young boys do: football, video games, trips out... We would compete with each other in everything, starting with our school grades but also when playing football or video games.

I realise that the competitive thing is fairly common but it was great because

ONE WOULD SPUR THE OTHER ON TO DO MORE AND MORE. THIS STAYED WITH ME, AS AN ATTITUDE TOWARDS LIFE. BECAUSE, IF YOU THINK ABOUT IT, MARCO SET HIMSELF AN INCREDIBLE GOAL AND THEN HE ACHIEVED IT.

I remember that as small kids, we must have been nine or ten, in the winter when we couldn't play football we had this go-kart racing video game demo, just two tracks and that was it. We'd spend the whole winter playing that game, checking our times, trying to improve with each performance. He was always totally focused; he was always like that, determined and tough.

Sport was everything when we were kids. Both in football and when we were racing in the European championship at 14, 15 years old, Marco was always the one who'd throw himself into it the most. Perhaps people were thinking: 'He should rein it in, he could get hurt', but nothing doing, he was the one who'd give it the most, while I am the opposite of him.

Coming home from high school each day became a race, from school to home and clearly there was no contest. I had my first motorino, which was quicker than his that still had a restrictor, so on the straight I had ten metres on him because mine was twice as fast but then he'd reach the corner and wham! he'd be in front of me. It was fantastic. He had a competitive spirit, a determination, tenacity... And he was also able to be completely different when racing to how he was in life.

MARCO CARES FOR YOU, HE'S NOT A BASTARD.

He was plucky, in everything he did. You bet on talent because you see talent is there but one also needs a determination and strength that not everyone has. I never saw him doubt himself. He's one of those people that always believe: 'I will give it my all', and it showed. There are times when you get disheartened, there are also times when you might doubt yourself, but he always had the strength to say: 'I put myself on the line, I give it my all'. And then he also had extraordinary talent, and so he was able to achieve what he wanted to.

In class we'd really play up. In middle school there was this design teacher, Borgese... He was one of those who'd leave you to it. He'd read the paper and of course the whole class would go nuts. Me, Marco and another kid, Samuele, were the ones that would always end up with a teacher's note. Every time we had a lesson, we got a note, nothing special, it was normal. We'd have pencil-case wars: each day at home you'd take the lids off your pens and each day there were ink marks and fights, we'd even get hurt sometimes. At primary school that didn't happen, we were better behaved. We were still supervised. I had my mum who'd keep me straight. In the afternoon we'd play football in the park, then he'd come to mine and we'd play on the PlayStation, always football games, there weren't any motorcycle games at the time. My mum would start to get worried, she'd call me telling me that I needed to eat and do my homework. She would always ask: 'Marco, do you want to eat?' and he'd say: 'No, no, I'll eat at home' and he'd stay and play while I had to go to the table. I would eat and he'd carry on playing alone in the living room. Great.

For as long as he was able to come to school every day, Marco always had good grades. Later, in the fourth year of high school, he rarely came and was the superstar, he could get away with doing what he wanted... Except when we had design homework: we would leave home with nothing and so in one hour, as well as getting the drawing done, we had to blag paper, square rulers, a pencil and everything else from our classmates. And it was fun when we were tested – Marco would be there at the teacher's desk with the book hidden, the teacher would ask questions and he'd be turning the pages trying to read...

Even after Marco stopped coming to school we organised a few dinners, as a class we were very close with friends from both middle school and high school. One time we were coming back from a party in Cesena, he was driving.

Another friend of ours was with us and he said: 'Come on Marco, do a bit of drifting on the road.'

'No, no, not on the road.'

We were in front of the Befane shopping centre and he insisted: 'Ok, then go in the Befane car park, maybe you can do it there.'

So we went to the car park, it was four in the morning, and Marco started skidding...

It was a BMW, his first car. He started skidding but at a certain point the security guard came out, terrorised, as if he'd just woken up. He was probably sleeping, at that time of night, and seeing these crazy kids... We left immediately but his face was priceless.

Sure, the bike was his life, the most important thing. Everyone sets objectives in life, there are things that you consider more important and then there is everything else. Of course, with the World Championship and everything we saw less of each other but I never thought: 'Oh, now he'll become a champion and everything will change'. Things happened to him but I always saw him as the same person, the same enthusiasm, the same desire to do, to fulfil himself, as if they were all different moments of his journey. He was always calm, yes, at times he'd get angry but only in so many words... he wouldn't get upset, that's how he was.

Supersic the champion and Marco Simoncelli the friend: there was never a difference between the two because you always had the same objective in front of you and over the years you did nothing but continue to move towards it with extreme determination and great success.

I always admired you. I would love to have the same strength in life to follow my goals. I'm still lost in the middle of nowhere while you entered the hearts of millions of people with your wins and your way of being. We don't play on the same field anymore, not in the same championship, not even at the same game.

It's not only you that has won Marco. You are now my teacher, my guide, the example that I want to follow.

Goodbye my friend.

Mattia Tombesi, 27 January 2012

SAMU
6
UNA TESTA DI CAZZO
[signature] *Simoncelli +1*
P.S. SKERZO

SAMU, U R A DICKHEAD,
BY MARCO SIMONCELLI
P.S. I'M KIDDING

FROM THE LEFT, MICHELE FUZZI, VALERIO MUCCIOLI, STEFANO GALLUZZI, SAMUELE CERICOLA, MARCO SIMONCELLI, MATTIA TOMBESI, ANDREA GIRASOLE **1999**

4. OFF TRACK

58
agv
RENTHAL
58
ACERBIS
aprilia
PIRELLI
ARROW
aprilia
HINSON

AT THE CAVA

PAOLO Maybe it was my fault because I'm the one that let him go. I should have said no, it's better not to do certain things when you're about to embark on something important.

It was Saturday and we were leaving the next day for Qatar, and the final test before the opening race of the 2009 championship. Marco was so hyped-up and despite all of his television commitments here, there and everywhere he'd worked hard, he was extremely prepared and ready to win his second World Championship. Instead we went to the Cava.

As usual the first run saw Vale and Marco battle it out, but that day Vale was stronger. The Cava is a very particular place and in addition Marco's bike wasn't right, but that day Vale had something more. At the end of the first race I said: 'Let's leave it there' but he and Vale insisted: 'No, let's do another one.' No sooner said than done, after two laps he was back, on the back of another bike, and when he showed me his hand I knew he'd broken the scaphoid. At that point I called the team in Qatar because the mechanics had already left and I told them that Marco was hurt. A cold shower for everyone, we desperately tried to contact Doctor Costa.

Marco had already broken his scaphoid in a 125 accident; that was also in Malaysia. Doctor Soragni had operated on him that time, in San Marino, it was thanks to him that we learned about the new way to operate; instead of a staple you use a self-tapping screw that with a non-invasive procedure takes the two pieces of that tiny bone and holds them firm, because the problem with the scaphoid, one of the eight small bones in the wrist, is that very little blood circulates there and so it never fuses. For a rider this is a big problem because the stress that is put on the arms and the wrists while braking and controlling the bike is huge.

We immediately decided to do the operation that Wednesday and a week later we went to Qatar to try to race, having missed the pre-championship tests. Costa was amazing, they tried everything and Marco wanted to ride in Friday's practice without painkillers.

The problem, I remember well, came on Saturday morning. We were in the hotel, he got up and said: 'Dad, this arm is really tired.' To which I replied: 'Marco if we race here we might risk missing Japan, it's in two weeks but in reality you have just a little over a week because you start riding on the Friday.' So Marco decided not to race and told Costa – Costa wasn't exactly happy about it.

That weekend in Qatar it rained hard, a total downpour in the desert! The only race that should have been cancelled was the 250 but in the end they ran a half race, delaying the MotoGP to the following day. In those cases they award half points. If we'd known that that would happen, perhaps he'd have been able to complete those ten laps, but when things start to go that way there's not much you can do about it. That year was born under a bad sign.

Marco was enthusiastic about everything he did, especially sport. All kinds. Once I was supposed to go and play a baseball tournament in Pesaro. Baseball, as you know, isn't played much in Italy, I learned to play when I was young and since then I've gone back to it every so often. Marco heard about the tournament and came to me: 'Lord, a baseball tournament, I'm coming to play too!' I was really pleased: 'Shit, great, but... why, do you know how to play baseball?'

'Yes, yes, of course!'

'Ok, cool, I'll sign you up!'

Then I thought for a minute: 'But when did you learn to play baseball? Where?'

'Well, I played it one morning at school, at middle school.'

So he'd played once for half a morning ten years earlier and, according to him, he knew how to play! Fuck that, I didn't sign him up! The same thing with tennis: 'I'm coming too, I'm coming too!' I didn't let him come, because maybe he'd even beat me... Can you imagine the embarrassment, losing to someone who's never played before!

He had great determination, Marco. I remember when Franco Morbidelli came to the Cava one time. He was a kid, racing in Stock 600, but he was really good. He was immediately quick there, and when someone has the speed, real talent may develop. He found himself there, competing with Vale and Marco; they were all there and Marco gave him an almighty shove to move him out of the way. He didn't say anything, poor thing. Afterwards I went to Marco, I was already laughing. He said: 'But shit, this kid rocks up, it's his first time... he has to understand where he's riding, he has to earn it!'

I was there too when the famous incident went down at the Cava, when Marco hurt himself just before the start of the 2009 World Championship. There are days when you go fast and then there are slower days, when you just don't have it. And that day Vale was in great form, almost unbeatable. They raced – Marco was taking crazy risks but still finished behind. It was already late and we'd already done a lot of riding, the following week the World Championship would begin... Anyway, Vale went: 'Ok, let's finish up'. And Marco: 'No, no, let's go again'. Paolo was also pushing to take him home but there was no way, he wouldn't budge. And so they had another race: Vale out in front again, him behind, desperate, and then he crashed out! We couldn't find the bike, after a while Marco came back up out of the ditch.

I met Sic in 2001, Roby Marchionni, the helmet guy, introduced us. At that time we'd go down to the Cava and at a certain point he started to come too with his dad, until one day Roby asked us if he could train with us there.

We told him he could and I remember that I even sold him my bike, I think he bought his first Yamaha 400 from me. We started training and, shit, in those early days Sic was really quite ugly. Over time he became cool but when he was small – I guess we all go through that ugly phase – he had these really long legs and really short body... basically he was still a bit awkward. When we started riding together he wasn't that quick, but that was normal – we had years more experience than he did.

But then he started to go fast.

WE HAD SO MUCH FUN AT THE CAVA, WE'D HAVE SO MANY FIGHTS TO THE DEATH ALSO BECAUSE WHEN YOU COMPETE WITH SIC IT'S ALWAYS TO THE DEATH, EVEN IF YOU'RE ONLY PLAYING POOL.

And we carried on like that, seeing each other mainly at races and at the Cava, at least at the start. Sic wasn't going too well, it was 2007 and he was in his second year of 250 racing. He had a factory bike but would crash a lot, make mistakes. And we started to see more of each other because he asked if he could come and train at Carlo's gym. So we talked about it, Carlo and me, to decide what to do, also because Carlo tended to watch over me. 'But if this kid ends up being your rival...' He was right but I thought Sic was a nice guy and I said: 'Come on, let's let him train here.' So he started coming to the gym almost every day, and from that point we'd see each other more often.

I also gave him a lot of advice, he was a big fan of mine and so he really listened to what I said. Then, coincidence or no coincidence, he went really well in 2008. We won the World Championship together, him in 250, me with the MotoGP and it was wonderful. He came to hug me during my lap of honour at Motegi, I went to hug him under the podium in Malaysia. It was great that we were both World Champions, and actually quite incredible that two guys that go to the same gym in Pesaro, both born in small towns a few kilometres from each other, both became World Champions together in important categories.

Valentino and I have some
great battles

We continued to be close friends from then on, and even started going to train together outside of the Cava, in all of our shared sports: motocross, flat-track, go-karting, we even invited him to do the Monza rally... Sic liked doing the things that I did and he was also a huge car fan: we spent a lot of time together.

When Sic hurt himself at the Cava, one week before the first race of 2009, I thought Paolo would kill him, he was so mad. That, there, was typical Simoncelli behaviour. Marco had turned up, we started to race and that day I was really fast. But there was always this competitiveness between us two... I was ahead, in a fast section, he was behind, and at one point he crashed badly, he basically folded the handlebar. The track was treacherous that day, there was a lot of water, it was soaking wet. I stopped but he was OK, even though he'd taken a big hit.

'Oh, Sic, all OK?'

'Uh, yes, lord, what a crash. Yes, yes, all OK,' he said.

We got back to the pits and his dad said: 'Son of a bitch, next week we're racing in Qatar, the championship's starting! If it was November... Right, enough, we're going home!'

He didn't back down: 'No, no, come on, don't worry.' There was no way to convince him to leave. 'Let's have another race!'

'No Sic, we'll just ride for a bit, no racing,' I said. His dad repeated: 'We're racing next week, you're always the same.'

But there was nothing doing, we had another race and, as before, I was in front, him behind and this time he crashed even harder, but I mean the bike went down in the river, we couldn't find it. He fell down, rolled for a while and, shit, we couldn't find Sic! He came back up, all white, and I thought: 'He must have hurt himself.' Yes, he had, and then he lost the 2009 championship. His dad was raging. If he could have bitten him...

Marco was like that: if he played at anything and didn't win, he'd always want to play again, and again, even if we were only playing pool. Sic was always very insistent: if someone didn't want to do something he'd have to tell him no at least 30 times.

He was good at football. His feet not so much... like me, but lord how he ran! He'd become a real athlete, Sic, he was so fast. We even played some games together with his friends or with my fan club's team but we had to stop because otherwise we'd argue... We did loads of things together, all kinds of sports. All good memories, we were a great group. With Pasini, Iannone sometimes, then Sanchio who'd become a close friend of Sic's. We'd go MX riding and Sanchio would bring the salami, red wine and sparkling water because he wasn't as fast as us and so he'd try to get us drunk. We saw another side of Sic right there – he was a pig, he'd eat like an animal. If there was salami he couldn't resist... 'Come on Sic, drink a couple of glasses of wine!' In the end Sanchio would get us drunk and beat us.

THERE WAS ALWAYS A CRAZY ATMOSPHERE AND A GOOD PART OF IT WAS CREATED BY SIC BECAUSE HE WOULD NEVER BACK DOWN WHEN IT CAME TO DOING STUPID THINGS. HE WAS A BORN MISCHIEF-MAKER, IT WAS HIS TALENT. BUT SHIT, HE WAS PURE. IF YOU KNEW SIC YOU LOVED HIM: HE WAS COOL, ESPECIALLY FOR THAT.

The biggest regret is that we weren't able to enjoy more time with him. All too often one of us would be busy, then the other the next time, and perhaps we wouldn't see each other for a bit. But you don't think about it at the time, because you can't imagine that you won't see him again.

When his book came out he gave me a copy with a dedication that said: 'Let's hope that, even if we become rivals, we will always stay friends.' That's how he saw it. I knew that we would end up like that, that he'd be my rival, it was no great surprise. I definitely didn't imagine it the first times I saw him, but when someone starts to make it in 250, going as fast as he did, winning the championship and coming close again the next year, you realise that he can become your rival. Also because he was nine years younger than me, he was the future.

He surprised me during that last year actually, because, yes, the Honda was fast but he had been extremely fast even if, at the end of the day, he hadn't got the results that he should have. At the start of the championship he should have been on the podium every race but he'd always crash. And fortunately he'd take out others too, so I was able to make up a couple of positions. Then, when we saw each other on Monday, I'd say: 'Well done Sic, thanks. Instead of finishing seventh I was fifth thanks to you!' And him, pissed off, with that voice of his: 'You're a shit, you're a dickhead, fuck off.'

I think Sic and I were similar in many ways. Some people said he would copy me, like in the way he dressed, he was yellow like me, but it was normal because he was part of our group, he got Aldo to do his helmet for example... In the end he was the new product to come out of our breeding ground.

HE WOULD HAVE BEEN MY SUCCESSOR: THEY LOVED HIM FOR THE WAY HE RACED, BECAUSE PEOPLE DON'T WANT TO SEE PERFECT RIDERS THAT SETTLE, THAT DON'T TRY. SIC, ON THE CONTRARY, TRIED RIGHT UNTIL THE END.

On the MX bike

SATURDAYS AT THE CAVA HAD BECOME A GREAT EVENT, FOR THE ATMOSPHERE, JUST TO BE THERE, FEELING WILD ON A BIKE, WHATEVER THE WEATHER.

Even in the cold, sometimes even in the snow... We'd get there and each of us would try to find the best set-up for his bike, mud, no mud... then we'd begin and battle would commence, even though in the end it was nearly always Vale and Marco fighting for the win. If I was having a good day I'd hang in there and be in the mix, other times I'd try and keep up only to finish on the ground.

Setting up the bikes was always fun because Marco was a perfectionist and so sometimes we'd wind him up.

'But, this bike, today...' he'd start, confused.

'Marco, it seems a bit slower today,' I'd tease him.

'Exactly, the bike's making me go wide today, maybe the fork needs another click...'

'Shit you're technical! A click of the fork at the Cava seems like a big step to make!'

Then maybe he'd go, crash, and I'd tell him: 'See, a click is too much, you need to be able to make a half click!' Professional tricks you see. So we had fun. Then we'd have the various finals and we'd finish with the highlight: salami, ribs and red wine.

THE GREAT THING IS THAT AT THE CAVA ONLY BIKE SPORT EXISTED. THERE WE WERE ALL THE SAME.

Marco, Valentino, me, Pasini when he was there, Paolo, Graziano Rossi, Aldo Drudi... along with other guys from Pesaro who'd come for the day with their MX bikes. There were no stars. There was no distinction, even if it was difficult to see a guy who makes salami for a living fighting against Marco or Vale.

But there was undoubtedly competitiveness; precisely because what we were doing there was sport. They were days of real motorcycling, that I think Marco needed in order to recharge the batteries far away from the pressures and stress of the World Championship. There at the Cava he only had to think about what he enjoyed doing: riding. And so he'd throw himself into it, while Paolo was the one trying to anchor him. But let's just say that he'd often, and willingly... cut the rope.

Once, for example, we'd just finished the second race of the day. I had stopped at the top of the bank as I wanted to do some filming. Then, I don't remember in what order, Marco arrived, and Vale, and Mattia. While we were chatting ('Hey, well done, you did it like that, I skidded...' etc) Paolo came along. It was already starting to get dark, it was cold and the day was almost over. At a certain point Marco piped up: 'Come on, let's make a couple of laps'.

And Paolo: 'I'd call it a day'.

'But no, come on, a couple of laps!'

'I'd call it a day'.

'Come on Paolo, don't bust our balls!' Marco said.

And Pasini turns round: 'Cool! I want to hear this, a kid telling his dad to piss off!'

And Paolo, without getting wound up: 'I give guys like you a kick up the ass from morning to night.'

What a scene.

Another great moment was when we let Marco stay at the top of the standings at the Cava for five whole minutes. He had missed the first two races with us because he was away testing in Malaysia with the team. Then he'd come back and, really fast, he'd won a couple of races and was back in the mix. After a couple of runs, he asked me: 'How are the standings?' He was all prepared, we knew that moment would arrive.

'You're first!' I told him.

'Impossible!'

'You are, you're first because we didn't count the races that you weren't here for!'

'Oh. Cool! I'm first!' Five minutes later someone came up to complain about a false start. I'd prepared a fake film clip with the images; you could see him start to move away before everyone else. 'But nooo, how... Shit, it's true though,' he couldn't believe it.

'Unfortunately they'll disqualify you Marco, so you were first for five minutes. Now you're second.'

'Lord, you guys are worse than the Spaniards!'

Those days spent at the Cava were so much fun that we had the idea to organise an actual charity event, an MX race at Cavallara, in 2009. This was because more and more people would come and watch at the Cava, we'd get there to find maybe five people and after 15 minutes we'd have to leave because there were already hundreds! So one time I threw the idea out: 'Why don't we channel all this enthusiasm, we'll all enjoy ourselves and we'll make money for charity?' And so we did it, inviting Dovizioso, Melandri and many others too. We tried to recreate the atmosphere from when we'd started out, going there in the camper, those old trucks. Most extraordinary of all was Kevin Schwantz's presence, a true legend!

When we thanked him at the end, with enthusiastic applause, he almost cried. It was an unbelievable day.

MARCO WAS, FOR ME, THE 'YOUNG OLD GUY', THE YOUNG GUY FROM ANOTHER TIME, BECAUSE HE WAS SO YOUNG BUT HAD THAT DESIRE TO LIVE AND BREATHE MOTORCYCLING AS I AND OTHERS OF MY GENERATION HAD HAD 20 YEARS BEFORE. THE SAME PASSION, THE SAME STRENGTH.

MAURO SANCHINI	IN THE CAR

I am a bit of a fanatic in the car: the temperature must be just so, this has to be like that, I never use the wipers because I don't like seeing the lines on the windscreen... Marco knew this and would enjoy winding me up. When we would stop he'd clean the mirrors with my toothbrush, saying that he was having fun, 'look at that', 'absolutely perfect', etc. Then, back in the car, maybe if I turned around for a second, he'd flick the wipers on with his finger... so annoying! The whole trip would be like that, cleaning it and making it dirty again, but still better than having him drive.

Once we had to go up to the mountains, to Malga Ciapela, Dino was there too. We met at 6.30pm to leave at 8pm, as usual, with this car bursting at the seams with skis... Marco drove the last leg, but so badly that he even made himself sick at one point! Just imagine how we were doing, with all the accelerating and braking. Dino, poor thing, was white, half dead, and I was the same up front.

One evening Erika and I were eating at Luciano's with Marco and Dino, we'd always meet up on a Monday or Tuesday, after races. We finished eating and Marco announced: 'Let's go and watch the race at my house.' It was already ten, it was starting to rain, but in the end we agreed: 'OK, let's go.'

At the first roundabout, the BMW was sideways, *bom, bom, bom*. Come on! At the second, the same thing, *bom, bom, bom*. And Erika asked me:

'BUT IS HE ALWAYS LIKE THAT?'
'ARE YOU KIDDING, THIS IS HIM DRIVING SAFELY!'

A right-hand turn, a left-hand turn, and we ended up in a ditch. Well not exactly in the ditch, the car was balanced precariously on the edge. We put the hazards on and we got out, all except Erika.

'Marco,' I told him, 'I think that if we touch anything in the car we won't be able to get it out again. Why don't you go to Paolo with Dino and see if we can find something to pull it out with?'

They headed off and some time passed, some people stopped to look and I downplayed it: 'It's nothing, a flat tyre, I'm a little on the edge, but it's all fine.' Marco and Dino finally came back.

'And?'

'Paolo told me to piss off.' But don't worry,' he added, 'I have an ACI card, we'll call them'.

The tow truck eventually showed up and pulled the car out. Between one thing and another it was now 1am. 'Marco,' I said, 'I don't think we're going to watch the race this evening.'

'Um, no.'

And Erika, who finally got out of the car, said: 'Oh, thanks for a great evening!'

MAURO SANCHINI   **MOMENTS**

I really enjoyed those nights, sometimes pretty late in the evening, when we would go running and Marco would share his feelings about the races. During the first year in MotoGP he was struggling to do the kind of times he wanted and we'd talk about it together. And every time he came back from a race it was like that: how he'd set the bike up, how he found it... 'Yes, this time it was better, we did this, we did that...' And he was always better, he was scarily good, he'd made that step up. Aside from his technical assessments, one of Marco's best qualities was his ability to listen to everyone, including me. As we ran, we'd talk. He knew that my experience could give him a push. Or, when I'd go and watch the races from the side of the track he'd always ask: 'Oh, how did I look?' And then he'd filter all the information that he considered useful.

A special talent of Marco's was to bring different generations together around him. We'd go for dinner and there'd be Paolo, from one generation, me from another, Marco who was even younger and maybe even some guys younger than him. And we'd all get on well together.

Marco took care of people, this was his gift. We went to ski in Livigno once; we were having a great time, so much fun... One day, chatting about this and that, I noticed I had a mole that seemed bigger than I remembered it. Vincenzo, a dermatologist and friend of ours, was there too and so I went over to him and said: 'Seeing as you're doing nothing, come here and look at this for me please.' Vincenzo took a look and said: 'Um, I think you need to get this checked right away, I don't like the look of it.' Marco, who was nearby, had heard us.

From that moment he started calling me every day to ask whether I'd been to get the mole checked. I went to get it seen to and they told me it needed to be removed. And Marco started calling me to ask when I was getting it removed. Once I'd done it they did some tests and saw that it was in fact a malignant melanoma, so Vincenzo, as a friend, told me: 'Listen, to be sure, we'll make a wider incision.' But I refused to budge: 'Listen, I don't want that. You know, I like cycling, riding MX, I don't want stitches. Let's leave it as it is.' Vincenzo talked about it with Marco and he started to bombard me again. In the end I decided to have that incision and I had to send him an mms with a picture of it to reassure him! I mean, it was a race weekend at Estoril, he had his own stuff to do right? But Marco always took an interest in others. On the human side he was devastating. And always, always smiling. Even in that press conference when Lorenzo had accused him of riding dirty, he said something like:

'OK, THEN THEY'LL ARREST ME.'

Fantastic.

One day, after the usual trip to the gym, Marco said: 'Come on, we need to put together a 250 film.' He was moving up to MotoGP and wanted to make a farewell DVD for all his mechanics, a wonderful gesture.

'Don't worry,' I said, 'I have everything. I'll come to you, we'll choose the clips and put it together.' Great. When I got there and opened the door I basically saw a big box with two legs behind it. He had a ton of VHS cassettes, not even DVDs! Free practices, qualifying sessions, races... everything!

'And now?' I asked.

'Now we'll watch them all and choose what we like!' OK. He put the first tape in, with the first race of the year, hit play and after 20 seconds he paused it. He'd seen an exit that he wasn't happy with. 'Look, here though... here I exited like this...' Then play. A few seconds later another pause, a static image, and we went forward like that, one frame at a time. In the end I had to take the remote off him. He would watch and re-watch everything, an unbelievable perfectionist.

“I LIKE RIDING THE MX BIKE, I LIKE RALLYING, I BASICALLY LIKE ANYTHING THAT HAS WHEELS AND AN ENGINE. ”

In 2009 we went to see the Superbikes at Monza, there were ten of us, all of us there on track without passes. The next day I went into a bar and heard: 'Oh, guess who we saw at the Superbike race yesterday? Simoncelli!'

'Oh yeah, Simoncelli?'

'Yeah, trackside! Him and those asshole friends of his! All trackside!'

I ignored it. I called Kate and said: 'I've just found out that we're assholes!', even though I knew that he hadn't said it in an offensive way, it was like saying 'that bunch of...'

AND SO IT WAS THAT WE BECAME SIC'S GROUP, THOSE ASSHOLE FRIENDS OF HIS.

We even made a banner for the Mugello GP with that written on it.

E GASSS!!!

THOSE ASSHOLE FRIENDS OF YOURS

QUEGLI STRONZI DEI TUOI AMICI...

QUEGLI STRONZI DEI TUOI AMICI...

BELTRAMO Here we are at Luciano's with Micky, Gianma, Dino, Kate...

MICKY Those asshole friends of his.

KATE He didn't want normal friends.

DINO I don't understand what the question is...

BELTRAMO There isn't a question, just tell us something about Marco for this book that Paolo and Rossella are doing.

GIANMA If Paolo and Rossella are going to read it let's avoid road accidents.

KATE And especially the reasons behind them.

DINO OK, so I can't talk about that time that we went to Ancona.

GIANMA We're running out of topics.

BELTRAMO Oh! Mattia's here.

DINO Pasini, the usual exhibitionist. Can you show a video in this book? It'd be a shame not to show his hair, look at him.

MATTIA It's because I haven't washed it, not because I wanted my hair like this.

DINO Nooo, the haircut! Pasini went to the hairdresser, sat down and as they started to cut he looked to see what he had in his pocket and said: 'Stop when you reach three euros.' And so he got that.

KATE Who was there that time, were you there?

MICKY Where?

DINO When Marco couldn't get his hair to fit under a cap anymore she cut his hair at a race!

KATE I cut his hair with the mechanics' clippers! It looked really crap, because my idea of a 'hair cut' was just take the hair and cut it, I wasn't measuring anything. Before practice he'd got really pissed off, saying he was hot and needed to cut his hair and I said: 'But you won't be less hot if you cut your hair.' 'No, you have to cut it for me.' It was in 250, in 2009 wasn't it? Ivan wasn't there, he picked a mechanic at random: 'Come here, cut my hair', so I said: 'No, OK, I'll do it for you'...

MICKY Afterwards he did his interviews with his helmet on because he looked so bad.

KATE The session finished, he went out, looked in the mirror: 'But look what you've done, I really look like shit!' and I replied: 'But I told you I shouldn't cut your hair, that I didn't have a clue what I was doing!' 'Kate, you could have cut it a bit better!' Oh fuck off.

DINO You didn't want to do it...

KATE Come on, his hair is all the same, it's not straight like mine, I couldn't exactly cut straight across.

GIANMA You needed to take that into consideration though as basically...

DINO But you didn't cut his hair dry did you?

KATE No, he wet it with the spray... I don't know, the water spray.

GIANMA Yes, the Glassex! Clear windows.

DINO With a squirt of Svitol lubricant!

KATE It didn't matter if it was wet or dry, the result would have been bad either way!

DINO You started underneath, wetting the hair...

KATE Yes, yes... you had to be there to see it! I was saying: 'But have I already cut here? Who knows.' A mess. So one part was shorter, one part longer, in fact he started using a hair elastic for a while, even if it was really short he'd tie it back with an elastic. He said: 'Never again, you're never cutting my hair again' and I said: 'It's not my job!'

DINO But anyway the result was still better than this one here!

(Luciano brings piadina)

MATTIA Have you talked about the dinner at Leo's?

MICKY It was Ferragosto, 13 August maybe.

GIANMA We'd gone to the coast, to play beach volley.

MICKY That's right... we'd had an aperitivo somewhere else. We were at Malindri. Were you there?

KATE I was about to ask you that.

MATTIA Anyway after an aperitivo, we were already merry, it was summer and we went to eat at this friend's house. Leo worked in the championship, a tyre man, and we went to his place, his new house... He really chose the wrong people to invite to his new house! We started in the garden, he was all smart, put together, Sabrina had cooked...

DINO Sabrina is his wife. At least she was his wife up until then, before the party...

MATTIA We started to eat and drink and then, who knows how or why, we started doing karaoke, singing really badly as we usually do. I don't remember who had the bright idea...

MICKY Who started it?

MATTIA I don't remember who did it, was it Kate?

KATE I said: 'Gianma, throw the water.' 'Shall I do it?' he asked. 'No, listen, don't throw it because then we won't stop.' I didn't have time to finish before he threw it, I don't remember at who, maybe Marco. 'Come on!' Everyone with a beer...

MATTIA Then we started emptying every glass that had something in it. Beer, wine, water...

GIANMA Even inside the house.

MATTIA The guy had only lived there a week...

GIANMA Then the party relocated.

MATTIA We got to Malindi, everything seemed pretty calm.

KATE Michele was asleep. I swear, he was sleeping!

MATTIA I sat down, Kate had a mojito.

KATE A strawberry caipiroska.

MATTIA Anyway, I showed up and Kate: 'Oh hi!' her glass moved a bit...

KATE I was wearing white trousers, you tipped the whole caipiroska over them!

MATTIA Only a drop!

KATE I wasn't thinking straight... I saw the mojito and bam! He turned around, he had mint...

MATTIA ... Mint running down me. The game turned into throwing mojitos. People were watching...

DINO Mojitos and fistfuls of sand!

KATE When the mojito was finished we started throwing glasses.

MATTIA And that evening I took a shower with Chanteclair degreaser! But were you there when we went to Fermignano?

DINO Yes! Straight to Malindi with the trucks!

MATTIA Because we went to train in Fermignano, then in the evening we stayed there, did a barbecue, it was so cool. Vale, Marco, Dino, my dad, they were all there...

DINO Uccio too, and Mauro...

MATTIA And Sanchio of course.

DINO Playing cards, drinking Montenegro.

MATTIA The great idea was to go to Malindi with the trucks, because it's on the beach. We'd park outside, unload the bikes and go down on the bikes. Then we must have come to our senses for a moment and we said no, we'd just go down with the trucks. And I said: 'If we only go with the trucks the challenge is to reverse into the car park.'

In Malindri's car park it's hard to park a Fiat 500 facing forwards. Marco had a Transit, I had the Daily.

DINO With the zebra print sofas inside.

MATTIA No, they're red!

DINO Red and zebra print, with zebra print cushions.

MATTIA Lord, that's all they had at the hardware store, I'll change it, OK?

DINO While Maria de Filippo was busy outside you took her van.

KATE Stop it!

MATTIA What was that German one Luciano?

LUCIANO I don't remember if you were there, when we met Vale and stopped to make a piada at the service station.

MATTIA Yes, because when Luciano came away he was always armed, in 2004 and 2005, when the paddock was still fun, we had the campers and travelled. Marco and I, for better or worse, were nearly always next to each other with the campers. And when Luciano came it was a joy because after a session you'd come in: 'Hey, come and eat a piada', piada with arugula and stracchino cheese, lord, you felt right at home, it was so cool. A couple of times we actually joined our campers together do you remember?

LUCIANO Vale and Uccio were there, we were going to Sachsenring. You were with Vale, you were going up together.

MATTIA I don't remember but anyway, Luciano is international with his piada.

GIANMA You know what made me laugh? He'd always talk about when they went driving with the white Opel with that guy, Brazzi…

MATTIA No, that was Matteoni.

KATE Don't use Brazzi's name in vain.

DINO Can't we say that everything goes? Shall we say we can talk about everything?

KATE No, Dino, not everything.

GIANMA I think I have to go now…

MATTIA And why do you two suddenly want to leave?

DINO I'll tell you later…

GIANMA I'm disassociating myself.

DINO You can't.

MICKY I'm leaving.

Sic's birthday

On holiday in California, our last, August 2011. We were in the car, me, Chiara, Michele and Marco, we needed to meet the others in the hotel at two and we only had ten minutes. We moved alongside Paolo and Marco said to him: 'We need an iPod cable'.

'Don't go and get it now, you don't have time, the others will have to wait around for you for half an hour...'

'No, come on, we're going to get it, we want the iPod cable so we can listen to music'.

'Marco, I said don't go, we need to all be here'.

Marco put it in first and set off. And you could hear Paolo: 'Why do I have a son like this? Why do you have to do this?'

Half way there Michele said: 'Come on, Paolo's pissed off, I could see he was pissed'.

We returned to our senses and headed back.

KATE RACES

Marco always told me that once he'd finished racing, he'd go and race cars with De Rosa. Those races that they do around towns, not illegal but dangerous and I thought: 'Right, sure, kill yourself doing that, leave me on my own.' I would imagine us at 45 years old, once he'd finished racing, like Capirossi now. What makes me sad is that I'll never see it.

RAFFAELE DE ROSA INTERPRETER

Marco would always interpret for me with Kate. And we were all speaking Italian right? It's just that she speaks Bergamo's dialect and I'm Neapolitan...

So he'd interpret for us: 'Look, he said this', 'Look, she said that.'

KATE	WHAM! SMACK!

We'd often go to Sardinia with Aligi, Elvio and the kids. So many funny things happened, like the episode of the fish that thought it was well hidden... we laughed a lot about that. We were snorkelling and there was this fish that didn't move at all. When we came out of the water, Aligi started: 'Did you see that fish that thought it was well camouflaged? If I'd had a gun I'd have harpooned it and laid it out right there'.

So Marco and Aligi started playing the part of the fish: 'Lord, look how well hidden I am!' 'Lord, no-one can see me! Wham! Harpooned.

That fish, even if you went up close, didn't move, he thought he was well hidden. We laughed like idiots.

Last summer we had a party at Chiara's agritourism.

Marco knew that he had to be the speaker that evening, and he and Michele were looking for the microphone. 'Chiara, where's the microphone?'

'Um, it should be up there.'

They found it, hooked it up and Marco started talking shit: 'If the DJ doesn't get any girls under the stage he'll kill himself.' He was the DJ. Chiara was well on the way to being drunk, she came back after 15 minutes and said to Marco: 'Hang on, I'll call my friend and attach the microphone, he knows everything, he knows how to do everything, he's great.'

MARCO ANSWERED HER THROUGH THE MICROPHONE: 'CHIARA, CHIARA!' WITH THE SPEAKERS RUMBLING, 'CHIARA, WE ALREADY HAVE THE MICROPHONE.'

But she's in another world, 'I'll call him for you, I'll sort it.'

'Chiara we already have the microphone!'

At one point we threw everything and everyone into the pool: everyone that arrived would end up in the pool. Even a laid table, we risked breaking everything...

They threw the sunbeds in too, we were surfing on the sunbeds, then they strung up a rope that crossed the pool and you had to walk across it and see who'd get furthest. It was impossible to take more than two steps and if anyone went back instead of going forward he'd hit his head on the wall... Everyone wanted to play that game of course, the most dangerous.

Alice arrived and asked me if I knew two guys who'd come from Livigno, two good looking guys, and she said: 'Shit, but what are they? Did they come out of that Marmalade Boy cartoon?' Because one was dark, the other blond.

Marco came over: 'What are you two sniggering about?'

'Nothing, we're not sniggering.'

But smack! he slapped Alice.

And she said: 'But what have I got to do with it?'

And him: 'You've always got something to do with it, so I'll do that and then we'll see.'

'But she's your girlfriend, I don't understand why I'm taking this.'

'Because I know you!'

Marco would always take the piss out of me and my girlfriends because we're from Bergamo. He would say that in Bergamo and Brescia we'd give it away like it wasn't ours...

Marco would sometimes call me in the middle of the night to tell me that they were ready to play billiards but needed a fourth guy. I'd get up and go to his house where they had the table I'd bought him and with one game, then another, we'd play till morning... Other times they'd stop here in the restaurant and play on my table.

When he'd come here you'd hear him because he'd drift on the roundabouts behind my place and you'd hear the tyres screeching. A neighbour of mine said to me:
'BUT WHO'S THIS MORON, DO YOU KNOW? I'VE SEEN HIM, IT LOOKS LIKE A GUY WITH CURLY HAIR.'

I'm a doctor and Marco was always worried that he had some illness. Every so often he'd ask me: 'Kia, that illness, what is it? Tell me about the symptoms?' I would tell him and then: 'Kia, I think I have that.'

The last time it happened was last summer in California. We were talking about a neurological disease, multiple sclerosis. Marco was interested to hear about the symptoms of the disease, so I told him. At the end of the evening, when we were alone, he said to me: 'Kia, I have to tell you something. I'm worried I have that disease.'

'Marco, are you nuts?'

'No, no, it's because I can feel my hands shaking.'

'Next thing we know you'll be going home and arranging to have an MRI!'

'Oh, you need an MRI to see it?'

'Yes, but don't go and do it!'

Five days later I called Kate, I needed to speak to Marco about something: 'Isn't Marco there Kate?'

'No he went to get an MRI.'

'I don't believe it!'

A week later Kate asked him: 'But Marco, why were you worried?'

'Look how my hands are shaking!' They were still.

He said to Kate: 'Show me yours.'

'No!'

In the end she showed him: 'Now this is a shaky hand!'

And Marco: 'You need to go and get an MRI!'

> **"YOU CAN'T ALWAYS GO FULL THROTTLE. "**

Marco taught me to ski in Carpegna, or rather him and his dad, because Marco didn't have much patience. 'I'll teach you, I'll do it', and after five seconds he'd already abandoned me, if I had to come down thanks to him I'd still be there now.

Once I bunked off school and we went skiing. We went to Ponte di Legno, Passo Tonale: me, him and all my friends from Bergamo.

I'd skied three or four times in my life, they took me to do a black run, telling me: 'No, you'll see, it's great, it's all flat'. I got up there, it was full of humps and the snow wasn't compacted down.

And Marco said: 'Don't worry, I'm behind you if you fall, I'll get your skis'.

Three seconds later two of my best friends had gone down fast, and he went after them, he had to pass them at all costs... So I'm there alone like a dick, and thank god some of their friends stayed behind me.

When I got down I looked at all three of them and said to Marco: 'Thank god you were the one who was meant to help me!'

And him: 'Um, you know, we had a moment... we weren't thinking straight, we started to go fast and I forgot about you.'

'Thanks!'

I would tell him: 'If one day you beat me on skis, I'll break them into pieces there and then and never ski again'. Marco always wanted to try and beat me, so one day we prepared the poles for the slalom and had a serious race, with the chronometer.

First lap: wearing my windjacket and trousers, I had three seconds on him.

Second lap: my advantage was a little less.

Third lap I tell myself: 'Maybe you should make a bit of an effort', and I took my jacket off. So did Marco.

The next lap I took my trousers off and Marco took something else off too. Then he said:

LORD, CHIARA, YOU DON'T NEED TO STRIP TO YOUR G-STRING JUST TO HAVE FOUR SECONDS ON ME! IF WE CARRY ON LIKE THIS I'M GOING TO BEAT YOU AND THAT'S THAT!

Presentation of our race
transportation

ROADS FULL OF SNOW

PAOLO That evening it was snowing like crazy in Riccione. We'd been in Viale Ceccarini, we'd eaten at Diana and as we returned home it was really snowing hard. But, with the roads full of snow and the four-wheel drive Audi A6, Marco was in his element.

He continued to complain that the problem with the Audi was the lack of a traditional hand brake, meaning he couldn't put it sideways, he couldn't correct it... I said: 'Don't bust my balls, just drive!' We got to a corner and the car slid, he was right, I can't even say he was going fast, the car skidded and we couldn't do anything because it had an electric hand brake. We found the only gap in a barrier of trees, we went through it and nearly rolled over. There was momentary dismay, also because we had three friends with us that weren't wearing seatbelts. We found that the real problem was getting out of the car because the Audi's doors are really heavy, it's very difficult to open a door from the inside when the car is vertical. The funny memory I have of that evening is of that idiot Dino who started to set off firecrackers! While I was as angry as hell and the other guy was dazed, they were all a bit like that, he pulls out firecrackers... I almost hit him.

Afterwards we had to take the three that were with us back home, so Marco took his mum's car, another four-wheel drive, and they went down into a ditch a kilometre further on. They told me that he said: 'No, this isn't happening. We need to pull it out, I can't ring my dad!'

THE CARIOLI RACE

PAOLO Last year I was contacted by a guy who asked me if Marco was interested in presenting the trophies at a carioli race that had already taken place the last couple of years in Coriano. As Marco had become famous they wanted him to go and present the prizes. Marco replied: 'But if I come, I come there to race'.

So we needed to find a cariolo kart. Round and round, we found out that Aligi used to do the Italian carioli championship. Aligi and Elvio pulled out two carioli: one was pretty much a wreck, the other was good so Marco of course chose the good one. The strange thing is that he'd never been on one before, the first test was one night at Coriano. The guys organising the event stopped the traffic, got in a car behind the cariolo with the headlights on to light the road and Marco, in front, went down, at full speed…

On the day of the race, it was 25 September, we got kitted up and Aligi came down from Bologna with some parts. Marione, his cousin, came too. We set up a 'garage' in the church courtyard and it was a great success. One month later we held his funeral in that same church.

That, I think, was the moment in which Marco really connected with Coriano, he became part of the town and the people understood who this boy really was.

The great thing is that he did the race and then came back up to the start line in a three-wheeled truck, a triumph. He stood in the back of the truck, hair blowing in the wind, everyone applauding him… it was really a wonderful moment. The problem with these carioli is that the races have become folkloristic, the rules are a bit fudged: Marco had a cariolo with ball-bearings but others turned up looking like true professionals, really kitted up. In the category in which the eventual winner was participating they didn't have carioli wheels but wheels from bicycles, karts, cars, so they were smoother and had better grip. Despite that, Marco set out to win, even if it was impossible. He recorded an amazing time anyway and finished sixth, saying: 'One more year and I'll win', making the changes he'd talked about of course.

That day he went around taking photos with the strangest carioli: the one that had won the race was made like a table, laid with glasses, wine bottle, plates… the wine was the hand brake, the chair was the seat, the glasses the steering wheel. Crazy, brilliant.

He took photos, he also did the prize-giving, he enjoyed the day, thinking: 'Next time we'll come and thrash them all.' That was his doctrine.

" I FEEL 'AGGRESSIVE', WITH INVERTED COMMAS. I RIDE THE BIKE A BIT IGNORANTLY TOO. "

'Karatella' race

RALLYING

PAOLO Gianni Cuzari had a wonderful office, one of those disorganised–organised offices, organised chaos let's say. I actually told him: 'This is the perfect office in which to swindle people.' Our participation in the Monza rally started right when we met Cuzari, who had come to GP in 2007 and seeing that Marco was going well in 250, he'd started to follow us a bit and offered him the chance to do the rally.

The Monza rally had become something of a show in the last years, and it was normal to put together teams with a driver and someone from the world of showbiz to be the navigator. First they gave us Cristiano Malgioglio: Marco would do his very first rally, in his very first race car, with this guy Malgioglio as his navigator, someone who I think knew very little about cars... Marco accepted but even Cuzari was convinced that he needed someone else, so he proposed Guido D'Amore, a wonderful person who really does do rallies, even World Championships; he raced for many years with Luigi Galli. Guido and Marco got on great, there was an immediate mutual understanding, the only difference between the two of them was that, in contrast to the racing that Marco was used to, in rallying precision is very important, you need to be really accurate.

I'm sure that if Guido D'Amore hadn't been there we wouldn't have done the first stage. Knowing Marco, and his slowness, his always being late, I went to Guido an hour before and said: 'Look, listen, get him to prepare a bit early because if you don't you won't start.'

This was how it went at first with this car, a diesel Uno. An extremely organised D'Amore and Marco, with his slightly disorganised way of doing things and the philosophy 'there's always time to get everything done'. That diesel Uno was really a joke, smoking every time you changed gear... But it was important because Marco learned to drive and was able to show his ability. So the year after, the approach was the same but the friendship ran deeper. We were able to have a Punto Super 2000 which was really fast and he proved that he knew how to drive, even Guido took me aside and told me: 'This guy is tough.'

When I met young Marco I was with my director general at the airport in Jerez de la Frontera. I was sat some distance away and I watched Marco and his dad, so close, it was really wonderful to see. I am a parent too and so I was particularly touched to see them talking and hugging together.

We started the rally thing with him in 2007, offering him a diesel Fiat Punto. Our main sponsor at the Monza rally was Metis, the same as Marco's team, and Piermario Donadoni, who I think saw it all as a bit of a joke, said to me: 'Shit, it would be a great publicity stunt to have Marco Simoncelli driving with Cristiano Malgioglio as navigator.'

'Come on Piermario,' I said, 'how can we put a driver of such calibre with someone showbiz? I think we should try and see how talented Marco is in the car.'

As I was also involved with Abarth at the time, I took Guido D'Amore, who is a professional navigator, and I put him next to Marco. And what a show it was! Marco would do things with that car... When Guido got out, after the first special stage, he said: 'Guys, this one has so much talent it's embarrassing, even on two extra wheels!' And the rallying game went from there. Marco got on with us and we stayed together for all of the future Monza rallies too. I've kept the photo that he and Paolo gave me at the last race, with the dedication: 'Thanks Gianni for all that you do, and I'll thank you even more if you get me a C4 WRC.'

Marco was so fast that in meetings afterwards with Guido we said:

'GUYS, WE SHOULD ENTER THIS ONE IN A MORE SERIOUS RALLY.'

And just like that we took the decision to go and do the rally around the hills of Cesena, the Colline di Cesena. We set off with the whole rag tag army – I think it was the start of 2009 because I have photos of Paolo, Martina and Marco on my truck from when we were celebrating his birthday – and I remember the awful weather, pouring rain... He would use the gears in the wet... if he'd had fifteen he'd have used them all. And he won, ahead of real rally drivers, people who knew the course by memory.

Marco came to Livigno three or four times. He was even confident on the ice... he was a real driver, 'driver' in the widest sense of the word, whether on two or four wheels. It was always fun with him because he had that desire to play, to joke, despite being extremely professional and serious. But when it was time to cause chaos Marco had a black belt, fifteenth dan. There must be thousands of anecdotes from the track: of jostles; of the time when the bonnet of his Ford WRC opened, breaking the glass, but he carried on anyway; or when he set fire to the clutch and got out of the car with the extinguisher to put it out... Maybe it's easy to say now but I have only great memories, as do we all.

My sporting and personal relationship with Marco began with a phone call before the first Monza rally that we'd be doing together. I am a navigator by profession and they'd chosen me to race with him.

I called him and he picked up: 'Guido... Guido, sorry but your name means bugger all to me...'

'I'm your navigator for the Monza rally.'

'Ah, lord, what a shit impression I've made...' and he laughed. 'You have to tell me how the notes work.'

'Don't worry, I'll see you at Monza in the morning, we can get to know each other and I'll explain it to you.'

I got there late in the morning under the usual Monza rally rain and Marco was already there with his camper. We met up and I immediately started explaining the notes to him. After a few minutes he said:

'GOOD LORD, THIS IS TOUGH, SHALL WE HAVE A PIADA?'

We set off for the race with the diesel Punto. He went through the first gears and said: 'It's slower than the 125... hehehe...'

By the end of the first stage he was getting to grips with everything and we moved on to the Grand Prix (the longest and most enjoyable stage, five laps of the track with all its normal turns and many tight chicanes made with traffic cones or tyres). A Subaru, much more powerful than our car, passed us. Marco stuck with him and I, realising the kind of trouble-maker I had beside me, said: 'Watch out, we don't have his brakes'.

Marco: 'Don't worry.'

MEDIA
ACTION

58

Super Sic

D'AMORE

T.

Tenuta

Lake Orta
Piemonte - Italy

BLUFF
www.blufftexas.com

"RALLYING IS A PASSION OF MINE. IT WOULD BE GREAT TO DO SOME RALLIES AT THE END OF MY CAREER. "

The outcome? The Subaru braked and turned, we went straight onto the run-off area, the car full of laughter. We tried again. After a few minutes the Punto seized up. Marco connected and disconnected the contact. We got to the pits and they asked him what happened: 'Lord, it died and so I jerked the isolator around like my dad used to do with the van and wow! It worked!'

The following year we raced with the Super 2000, a more powerful car.

After a great race he said to me: 'Lord, Guido, if you took an idiot and turned it into a car, you'd have the Punto!' That same year we did the Colline di Cesena, a minor rally but very difficult if you have to do it in the snow as we had to. In those conditions, if you have to choose a car, avoid the Punto. Marco was nevertheless able to record some amazing times, a real rally talent.

The year of the Ford Focus WRC – the top category, that of the World Championship – I remember that we were busy doing the usual Grand Prix stage when the Focus started drifting dramatically and Marco: 'Wowwwwwwwwwww! Like the real ones, did you see?'

We got to the pits and spoke with the car's engineer about set-up for the next stage. We were all concentrating on strategy, Marco turned around and said: 'I think it's fine as it is, I'm going to cut my nails'.

We started the stage and hit a section of safety fence, New Jersey or something. The wheel span suddenly and Marco hurt his hand.

I was quick to say: 'Don't push it, think about your career'.

'Lord, rather I'll finish with only one hand...'

I miss my 'trouble-making friend' so much, and when you share a cockpit you create a special bond... it was really great with him, I often think about the fact that everyone's seen him race from the outside but I've had the privilege to see him race next to me.

On four wheels

> **❝ FORMULA 1 WOULD BE A GREAT EXPERIENCE, BUT RALLYING IS MORE VARIED, IT CAN BE MORE FUN. ❞**

We woke up to girls a little late in the day, but when we were 15, 16, we'd go out and end up in Viale Ceccarini. We'd try it on with foreign girls, we'd developed a strategy. We had an agreement with Andrea Girasole's dad who had a restaurant and bar and, if we managed to find a group of girls, he'd bring us all shots to drink.

WE TOLD THEM IT WAS VODKA BUT OURS WERE IN FACT JUST WATER... SO THEY'D GET DRUNK AND WE'D STAY NICE AND ALERT!

One time there was me, Marco, Andrea and Samuele, we'd seen these four girls, a bit older than us. They weren't very flirty but we offered them drinks. They did a couple of rounds with neat vodka, while we drank water as usual. At a certain point they asked for strawberry liquor, a totally different colour, and Andrea's dad couldn't give it to us... So he brought us water anyway. But they got suspicious, they said to one of us, 'Let's taste it', and so we were rumbled and they left, pissed off.

What a strategy... it never worked very well but it was fun.

I remember Marco's first kiss! It was for a bet, who kissed better, him or Girasole. We were on a coach, coming back from a trip with one of our female classmates from middle school. Later on he had more luck with girls but at the start they weren't bothered and neither was he really.

When we went to Peter Pan he was a bit impatient because everyone there is so trendy, people from Riccione are like that... He had no time for that world which was understandable, and he wouldn't go to those places. I don't know, at 16, 17, maybe even younger, you dress like this and you do your hair like that and you go to certain places to be cool, but he was not like that at all, he couldn't have cared less.

He was already famous one of the last times that we went to Peter Pan, it was full of people who loved him. You could see he was a bit annoyed but he still made time for people. If I was him I'd have been ten times more angry, also because as you move around there are people that touch you, talk to you and they're not always all friendly. Or maybe you come across the drunk guy... But Marco was probably used to it by then and was able to keep calm and not get wound up.

Our first New Year in Bormio, I was working at the club there and Marco came up with me. They'd given us the 'PR house', with no heating! There were nine of us and we were freezing.

I HAD LOADS OF FRIENDS IN BORMIO AND SO EACH EVENING A NEW GIRL WOULD ARRIVE, THERE WERE SO MANY, GIRLS, GIRLS, GIRLS...

On New Year's Day, at 6.30am, we took the last cable car to the truck making sausage sandwiches. There were loads of people there, they all recognised Marco. Eventually the sausage was ready. We crossed the street to head back, he went to take a bite... and was left with the bread in his hand while the whole sausage fell into a puddle of snow at the side of the road, disgusting. So Marco picked up the sausage, looked around as if to say: 'Let's see if they see me' (in fact everyone was staring), feigned ignorance and put it back in the sandwich.

As I'd worked on the 31st, me and the guys from the organisation wanted to celebrate the day after so I left Marco and some other guys and female friends of mine at home and I went out. I got home at 3am to find lights on in the kitchen, a mess. I opened the door and saw seven completely naked girls, three of my mates, half dressed, and Marco, who'd discovered Moon Boots that year and loved them – he was naked with his Moon Boots on. 'He was the first to lose every hand of poker', they told me. He'd lost them all on purpose!

> " A BIKE ATTRACTS CHICKS LIKE A PIADINA ATTRACTS CHEESE. "

In 2008, on holiday in Formentera, he wore a hair elastic:

'SHIT, MARCO, YOU LOOK GREAT WITH A HAIR ELASTIC',

because it showed his forehead. He'd become good looking but as a kid no-one looked at him and we would throw fuel on the fire: 'Come on Marco, we'll send that girl over to you, we'll convince her.' With two words these girls here started to notice him.

Once we were in one of the beach bars in Riccione, and there was a cute girl behind him, a redhead.

We said: 'But that's Simoncelli!'

And she: 'No, no, it's not him.'

So we called to him: 'Excuse me, aren't you the guy who races in 125?'

And he, all embarrassed: 'Come on, stop it!'

'No, no, it's you, I recognise you!'

Then we left him there to talk with the girl. She was really beautiful, red hair, blue eyes... I wandered off and when I came back Marco was alone. The day after he told me:

'Anyway that girl I was talking too said "Your cousin's cute!"'

'Are you nuts? You want to wait a week to tell me?'

Another time, he was in 125, maybe the first year, after a massive party in the nightclub where I was working in Monza, we went home with two girls, to their place. I was out on the terrace with one, Marco goes into the bedroom with the other.

Months before, him and me had been going out with two girls. Marco got on really well with this girl who was called Federica and he'd always ask me: 'How's Federica? Fede, Fede, Fede', when we'd speak to each other he'd drive me nuts with talk of Fede.

So that evening after the party I went in off the terrace and thought: 'Let's see what this idiot's up to.' I went towards the door, left ajar, and heard this phrase, I was laughing so hard inside:

'COME ON FEDE, TAKE YOUR PANTS OFF.'
'BUT MY NAME'S CARLA!'
'OH. WELL TAKE THEM OFF ANYWAY!'

But that time in Formentera, when I met the girl from Turin, Marco was already famous. I was there with this girl who said: 'I heard that Simoncelli's around'.

'Who the hell's Simoncelli?' We pretended not to know each other, sometimes we'd have fun with this joke!

'A guy who races bikes, with curly hair... that guy there!'

'I think they're pulling your leg, I've never seen that guy before'.

At a certain point Marco saw me: 'Oh, let's go and get a drink!'

The girl looked at him and said to me: 'But is he crazy? He doesn't know you and he takes you for a drink?'

'Um, who knows what's going on in his head... Riders...'

How we'd laugh creating these scenes...

I KOHE
BELLA GALLINA

AND HOW CAN I RESIST TOUCHING YOU? YOU MAKE ME FEEL AS HORNY AS A CHEETAH. CIAO PRETTY CHICKEN, BY MARCO SIMONCELLI

When Marco and I went out together we were trouble. But then often it'd be just the two of us and he'd share difficult times with me. It wasn't all parties, craziness and drifting: when these difficult moments came I was aware of it because he was quiet.

When the accident with Pedrosa happened in 2011 Marco was really down. He knew he'd messed up trying to pass through that turn at Le Mans when he could have waited for the next one, but he was convinced that, if he managed it, the crowd would stand up and cheer. He didn't manage it, but if he had... Above all he was upset because Pedrosa had broken his collarbone. So he sent him a message that he let me read. When he realised that Pedrosa would never answer, it bothered him, and he didn't understand why he wouldn't shake his hand the next time they saw each other. But Marco was like that: no messing round, he wanted to pass him there. This flair, this madness made him different to everyone else, that pinch of crazy had got him where he was. People felt it and loved him for it. He would have been perfect to race with those guys, those guys from another time: Rainey, Gardner, Schwantz, Doohan...

Marco had a big heart and a beautiful soul but also a brain – he was intelligent and inquisitive. Sometimes we'd stay at his parents' house and talk politics, economics... he was interested in everything, he'd ask, want to learn, have an opinion. Especially with things he knew nothing about. Not that he was perfect, he had his defects, he was impulsive, but he wanted to understand, he would think.

My girlfriend would sometimes bust my balls, she was a bit jealous, particularly about the time we'd spend together. But that friendship, like all friendships, was a type of love. Marco and I would speak every day and when he was at home we'd see a lot of each other, even if we had nothing planned. I'd go to his place, we'd play cards, watch a film. We'd eat what we had, what he was eating. Once, at 2am, I wanted to go home and sleep because I had to work the next day. But Marco, knowing I lived alone, said:

'WHAT THE HELL ARE YOU GOING HOME FOR? SLEEP HERE, I'LL RENT YOU A ROOM!'

5. THE JAGUAR

I would see Marco at the Cava and I knew that he was a young rider that many people were talking about, they said he was fast. He was always with his dad and we'd say hi to each other and that was it, because they weren't very chatty and also because Paolo had a mean face and so I stayed away. But I saw this tall kid, who was growing and didn't walk to a beat, he moved in a strange way… and I asked myself: 'Shit, but how can a guy like that be fast? Motorcycling is all about rhythm, harmony.'

One day a mutual friend called me and told me that Simoncelli wanted to ask me to do his helmet for the following year. So Paolo and Marco came to see me and said: 'You're a professional and we've come to work with you, no mucking around, we need to do the helmet.'

THE STORY BEGAN THERE BECAUSE WITH MARCO INVOLVEMENT BECOMES ABSOLUTE – HIS ADVENTURE BECOMES YOURS TO A CERTAIN EXTENT.

Working together with Marco and Paolo meant that we became more than friends.

The first helmets were based on what I saw as being very complicated graphics, but right for 250 because in 125 the kids want more creative graphics, then in 250 you try to clean it up a bit so that when you get to MotoGP you find the essence, like we found with Marco.

THE WHITE HELMET WITH THE TWO RED LINES WAS, I THINK, ONE OF MY BEST PIECES OF WORK. A HELMET FOR A RIDER FROM ANOTHER ERA, VERY RECOGNISABLE.

I had trouble convincing him. Marco was one of those guys that would immediately speak his mind if he had doubts but at the same time he would listen to every suggestion. He thought about it and said: 'Shit, it is beautiful you know?'

At the start someone told me that Marco wanted to imitate Valentino. But as soon as I knew him better I could clearly see that his style was totally different. Both in life, and in his approach to racing, to everything he did. But like Valentino he was fastidious; he didn't leave anything to chance. He had all his obsessions, his graphics, his things that would really psych him up, he loved them deeply and once he decided to use something it became his.

Like the jaguar. When I asked him why he'd chosen the jaguar he told me that he thought it was the calmest animal in the world, laid out on a branch because it's hot, he stays there, not wanting to do a thing. But then, when they wind him up you better watch out because he's one of the most unpredictable animals.

There was a reason behind everything, from the colour to the theme of the graphi[c]t's like that for all of the fast riders I've known over the years, Doohan, Schwant[z] Rossi: they're very aware of what they wear, it's really like a bullfighters costume fo[r] them. They have great respect for their own image, I think it's psychological. It helps to exorcise fear, make an impression on their rivals, it's an age-old story.

This is the thing I like the most, because it means that my job is not only to pain[t] things, perhaps there's more to it. And with Marco the return was unbelievable. He was an old-school rider. I think that when he watched those Villeneuve tapes he wasn't watching Formula 1 but the act. He loved the knightly, glorious act. This was his character, his way of racing, what brought him to success. But it wasn't easy, it was a hard slog, because that winter in 250 when he got landed with the unofficial bike fo[r] the second time, Marco was really cut up

[I] remember when we were talking with him and Paolo about the famous Pedros[a] incident at Le Mans. Paolo continued to say, 'Look, you were closing the gap, he shouldn't have resisted' and Marco said, 'No dad, come on...' Because we criticised him we told him, 'Shit, you could have waited, you would have left him there at the next turn anyway.' And so when Paolo started justifying it Marco replied: 'No, dad, lord, shit, come on, I went too far, I went too far!' Then, during a pause, general silence, he started up again: 'You know what? When I came off the brakes I thought, lord, now I'm going round him on the outside, you'll see!'

Marco was great, rough round the edges but smart, he was extraordinary. He would also cause chaos: he'd roll up and start to leave everything everywhere, his fleece, his keys, he'd put everything down and in two minutes the office would be full of his stuff that he would of course then forget, he would have to go up and down the stairs three times, first for his keys, then for his bum bag...

He'd come here three or four times a week just for the fun of spending time with us. That final summer, during the first hot days, he did the funniest thing. We heard the bell ring, opened up and Marco ran in, all sweaty, with his jet helmet on and open.

'Sic, what the hell are you doing here?' I asked him.

And he said: 'Listen, I have to take a shit! I had to decide whether to do it here or at my grandma's! My grandma lives behind your place, but then I thought well, we're friends, I'll do it here!' He went to the bathroom, then said bye and went back down the stairs!

Another great thing, we'd started watching some '70s films together. One evening with his friends, we put on *The Treasure of San Gennaro*, with Nino Manfredi and Sent[a]

Berger. She was a huge sex symbol! We'd die laughing because he loved that type of comedy, he'd watch Totò too.

Every Sunday, after the races and after eating a piadina, he'd review things. He was extremely critical of himself and had a very correct way of seeing things, he'd never say: 'The bike's not right' but rather 'I made a mistake'. But then the ending was always the same: 'Anyway Sunday I'll go there' – to the next race – 'lord, I'll open the gas and fuck off, I'll show them!'

'FUCK OFF' WAS HIS WAY OF CLOSING, HIS STAMP, IT SUMMED UP HIS VITALITY, FOR EXAMPLE WHEN HE LEFT HE'D SAY: 'OH GUYS, I'M OFF. YOU KNOW WHAT? FUCK OFF!'

Last year there was also the trouble at Barcelona and once again, before he left for the track, Sic had said: 'Now I'll go there and fuck off!'

We were really worried and said: 'If he does the same thing again there...'

And so everyone tried to calm him down. We got to Barcelona and he took pole, amazing! I remember that I was in Ducati's hospitality unit that evening, I was having something to eat with Valentino and the other guys, and I saw Sic arrive. So he and Vale shared their impressions of practice and Vale said to him: 'Oh, tomorrow, don't go in front, stay on Stoner's arse and if you sit there he'll go nuts'. He could sense it was going to be a strange race.

And he looked at him, as if to say, 'Shit!'

The day after Marco said to me: 'Lord, Valentino Rossi told me to stay on Stoner's arse! You see where we've ended up?'

Every so often I too would try to make him realise the level he'd reached, 'Do you understand where you are and what you're doing or not?' It was almost as if he didn't realise, he had no airs at all.

One time I went to Misano to make some laps with friends and at four in the afternoon Sic arrived, dressed in typical Sic style, on the MV Brutale. At one point he was there, going along the straight with the Brutale up on one wheel, he'd look at you with the bike weaving and then bang! He put it down, made the front wheel smoke and threw it into the corner, a twist of the throttle and sideways into the Quercia and then he stopped. 'Did you see? Did you see that slide?' Pure show. Amazing! He really had that sense of showmanship. The Brutale was really small considering, you know, how big he was!

Another time we went to eat at Bibo, a bar on the seafront, where the road racing track once ran. As the bike wouldn't start he said: 'I'll do a push start!' They'd do push starts here! So he starts up this Brutale in front of the kids' trampolines, with the restaurant full of people, and gives it some gas, a cloud of dust, shit!

One thing that I'd always rub in his face was that there was a period in which I used to beat him, when he was a kid and I was younger, we'd ride at the Cava and I was quicker than him. I even kept the paper with the standings, any time he'd bust my balls I'd pull out that paper and say: 'Oh, shut your mouth!'

One thing that he rubbed in my face was the fact that I wasn't there when he won the 250 World Championship in Malaysia. I'd promised him that I'd bring him a glass of water at the end of the race, because he was always sweating. 'Hey, you were meant to bring me water, shithead, you weren't there!' I remember that in Spain, when he won, I took him that glass of water that he drank straight away at the side of the track... It sounds like a stupid thing, but it was really great.

THE REAL ADDED VALUE WITH SIC WAS HIS FAMILY, TO A GREAT EXTENT HIS FATHER PAOLO AND TO AN EVEN GREATER EXTENT HIS MOTHER ROSSELLA, WHO ALWAYS HAD THE FINAL SAY.

He was deeply honest, Sic. He was always able to see the good in others; he wasn't aggressive or resentful as some had said. And this was why I fell in love with Sic. Sic was, for me, my granddad: you'd never argue with your granddad, you'd never start that kind of discussion because after all he's your granddad. And when he'd hug me, because he was a very affectionate person, it was as if I was hugging my granddad. Because he was reassuring, when it came to the important things he was as reassuring as nature, like a tree. When Sic would hug you it was like when, in summer, you put your arms around a big tree, warmed by the sun, and you feel something go through you...

| ANDREA DOVIZIOSO | THE SAME DREAM |

Marco and I always had a strange relationship.
WE WERE ALWAYS SO DIFFERENT, BUT WE FOUGHT THE SAME BATTLE, WE HAD THE SAME OBJECTIVE, WE CHASED THE SAME DREAM. AND THE SAME DREAM CAN'T EXIST FOR TWO PEOPLE...

Marco was my opposite in many ways. He was much more of a joker, much more instinctive, much less precise... I always respected him but I never shared his way of racing – his sense of risk was different to everyone else's, and even more different to mine. I had realised this right back in the second Italian minibike championship. He didn't consider the dangers, he didn't think, he'd throw himself in and that was that. When he decided to pass there was no plan B. And he didn't care whether it was possible or not, he'd try anyway. He'd pass and that was that.

But when you're going fast you need to consider a load of variables. If you decide to go for it, a few seconds pass before you start your attack. That's normal. And in those seconds everything can change, the most likely thing is that the other rider will try everything to prevent you from passing, and when that happens there's trouble because you want to move into a space that's not there anymore.

The passion that he put into everything caused him to make mistakes, to risk big. But in the end the mistakes paid off as he was able to win the 250 championship, go extremely fast with a 250 (few in the world are able to go really fast) and reach MotoGP.

Marco was only one year younger than me, but we'd developed in very different ways because he, instinctive and throwing himself into things, often found himself in trouble. So his career had seen some breaks, some delays while I gradually came up, step by step, through the categories. He would always catch up to me when I was about to be promoted to the next category but it was always a disaster to have to battle against him. Finding myself up against Marco was a nightmare that returned regularly, he was with me throughout my career, minibikes, Italian GP, 125 World Championship, 250 and MotoGP – we raced in all the categories and on all bikes, though never for more than two years at a time. But then, after GP, there were no more categories, we were both at the top of the top.

In Simoncelli I always saw a rider with great talent that could have beaten me in the future. But in truth, in all these years he'd only done it once, in a minibike championship when he was seven. And that was it. I think he too considered me a stronger rider. The fact is that he was always considered to be like me, or better than me, in those last years in MotoGP. As if he had the same chance of winning a world title. This was something that affected my self-confidence and that became almost an obsession for me.

I could lose to a Valentino, a Pedrosa, a Stoner, a Lorenzo and I'd still sleep at night. BUT MARCO WOULD KEEP ME AWAKE, PARTLY BECAUSE I WAS SCARED, PARTLY BECAUSE EVERYONE BELIEVED IN HIM MORE THAN THEY BELIEVED IN ME.

Maybe it was because he had that warrior-like quality, pushing and going fast which meant that even if he finished behind in the championship, he still made more of an impression.

WHOEVER BATTLED WITH SIMONCELLI HAD TO ADAPT TO SIMONCELLI. YET IF I FIGHT WITH CASEY STONER I DON'T HAVE TO ADAPT TO CASEY – I BRAKE HARD AND THEN SEE WHAT I HAVE TO DO. BUT IF I HAD SIMONCELLI BEHIND ME I COULDN'T BRAKE HARD BECAUSE HE'D ATTACK, I KNEW HE'D TRY TO PASS. SO I HAD TO SLOW DOWN, TO CONTROL HIM. HAVING TO ADAPT TO A RIDER, SHIT, IT'S NOT FOR EVERYONE. BUT HE'S ANNOYING, REALLY ANNOYING, AS A RIVAL.

Despite our rivalry I knew that Marco was a good guy. As kids we'd fight like crazy but then, once it was all over, we'd play football together. We didn't humiliate each other, we'd play. You could always see that he wasn't one of those sons of a bitch that would get a kick out of it if you lost or if something happened to you. No. If you hurt him, his eyes would get small, like a cat. And this doesn't happen to sons of a bitch. But then rivalry means that you don't share anything, you get lost in the bullshit. And this, if I think about it, is a huge shame, unforgivable.

| VALENTINO ROSSI | EVERYTHING AND A LITTLE MORE |

Over the years it's true, we became rivals too, because Sic had grown. Towards the end of his first year in MotoGP he'd started to go fast and it was a pity that I'd gone to Ducati with all of the problems that that brought, because when he became fast I started to suck which meant there was never a real battle like we'd had at the Cava, fighting for the positions that counted on the final lap. It was a shame, it would have been fun.

He was very sweet in much of his behaviour. But he was also ignorant, stubborn and on track, shit, even if you were his friend he'd always bust your balls.

Carlo always told him: 'There's one thing you haven't understood Sic – for you motorsport is a contact sport, like football. But it shouldn't really be like that.'

But I think that he thought: 'I'm a giant compared to the others. I have disadvantages compared to these dwarfs but at least I can make my kilos count when there's a "full contact" battle.'

Anyway, fighting against him was really great... OK, he was a guy who'd make cock-ups, like for example the error with Pedrosa, but the other riders, especially Stoner and Lorenzo, picked on him because they were scared of him. Because Sic, at times,

> "WHEN I WAS RACING MINIBIKES VALE HAD STARTED IN 125, AND I WAS A FAN OF HIS. BASICALLY HE'S ALWAYS BEEN A REFERENCE POINT AND REACHING THE POINT WHERE I RACE AGAINST HIM IS GREAT, EVEN MORE SO IF I CAN GET IN FRONT OF HIM."

You've pissed me off Vale

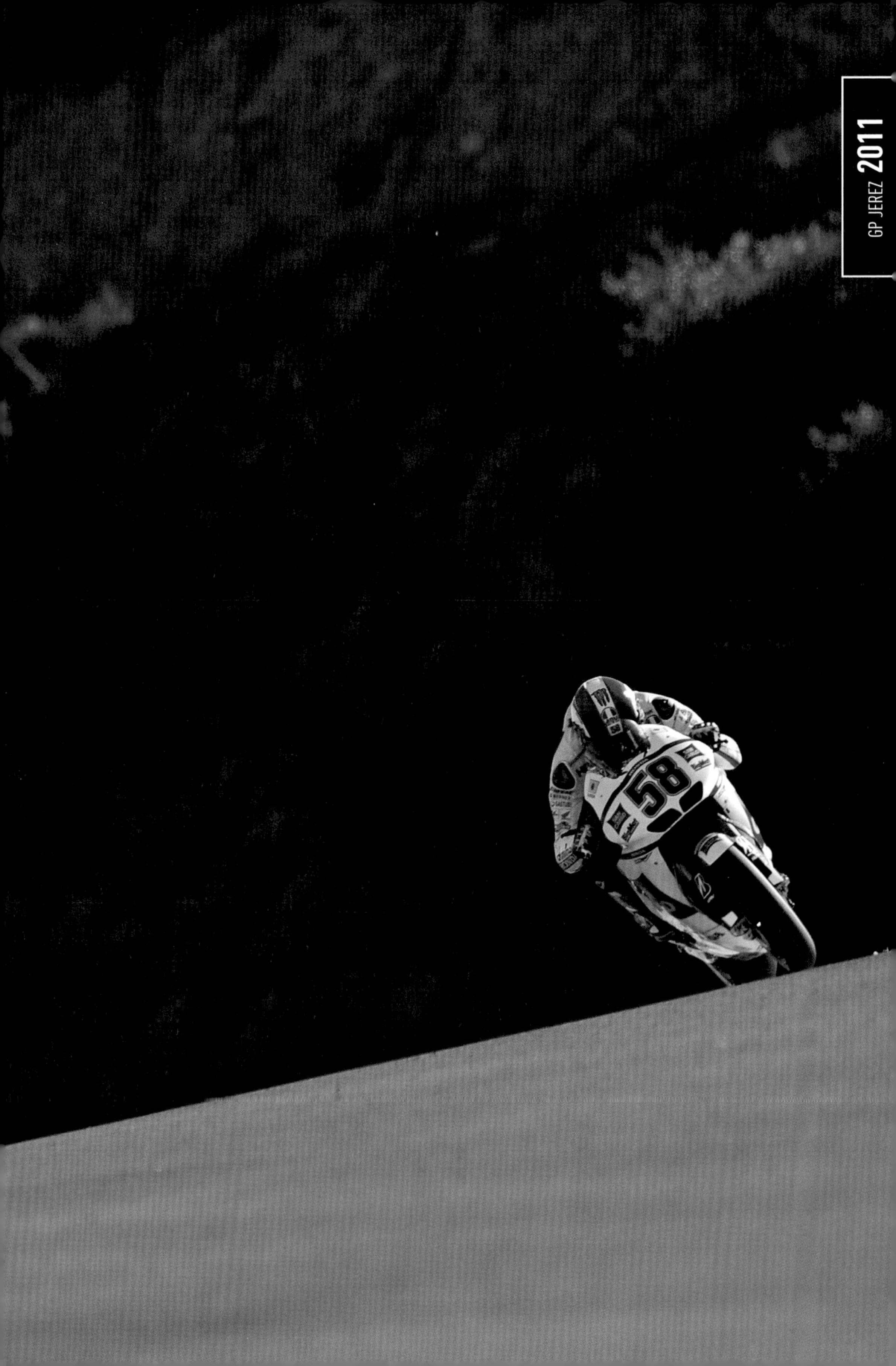

was a little out of line but bike racing is also like that, almost anything goes on the last lap.

And in 2011 he was often very fast.

IN THE END YOU'D SEE HIM AND THINK HE WAS A DICKHEAD, BUT HAVING EXPERIENCED HIM CLOSE-UP I CAN SAY THAT HE WAS A PROFESSIONAL, HE WOULD TRAIN HARD, AND ABOVE ALL HE KNEW WHERE HE WANTED TO GET TO. HIS OBJECTIVE WAS ALWAYS TO GIVE IT EVERYTHING. AND A LITTLE MORE.

He was pretty reckless in some ways, like when he went drifting. As soon as he got his licence he had five or six accidents one after another, in the space of three, four months. Then he calmed down. Sure, he'd arrive and say: 'Lord, I was drifting there at the exit.' You'd answer: 'Shit Sic, but that turn there, if you haven't yet got the hang of the car it's too dangerous to drift!' He would say you were right, because that's what he'd do, but then three days later he'd go and crash again, at that same turn. Because he wanted to try, right? And maybe he wanted to show that he could do it, even if he had to make more than one attempt.

Sic had an old-timer's approach to battling: friends, friends, friends my arse!
On the track he was like that. Sometimes off track too. He was inflexible towards those who pissed him off.

Many people tried to create trouble between Sic and me. Many went to him and said: 'Ah but you'll see that when you get in front of Valentino, he won't be your friend anymore.'

To me they said: 'Ah, because he plays dirty, he's doing that to learn your secrets...' All this bullshit.

BUT WE ALWAYS GOT ON REALLY WELL, THANKS ESPECIALLY TO HIM. YOU COULD REALLY SEE THAT HE CARED ABOUT ME. HE WAS GENUINE. AND THIS WAS WHAT MADE THE MOST DIFFERENCE, AND WHAT REMAINED, EVEN LATER, ONCE WE BECAME RIVALS.

Only me, him, Carlo, his dad and maybe his mum understood our relationship, no-one else, not even his girlfriend. He was really a fan of mine. He had grown up watching my races, so you could see that for him it was always a real privilege when we were together. On the other side, of course, we were friends on the same level.

I had so much fun with Sic. When I broke my leg he came to see me many times, and once he came with Kate, from the coast, and we spent time together. Those are the things that unfortunately you only really appreciate later on. You think about it and say: 'Shit, that was cool.' Because in the end, apart from my closest friends, many came to see me just once while he would come running whenever he had some time. We wouldn't do anything much, he'd keep me company, we'd watch the matches. It was great, you could tell that he did it just because he wanted to do it, not because he had to do you a favour.

> ## " MOTORCYCLISTS? WONDERFULLY STRANGE PEOPLE. "

MAURO SANCHINI   WE DID SOMETHING STUPID

One day, we were training together (Marco would always challenge me to races and he'd kill me, with those long, muscular legs of his) and he threw out: 'Oh, come to Mugello next week, I have to go and test the Aprilia RSV4, because they've asked me to do the Superbike race.' He was meant to race at Imola, he'd never seen the track, never used Pirelli tyres, never ridden a Superbike.

'What do you mean the Superbike race?'

'Yes, yes, Aprilia wants me to go, I would like to – it's a good experience...'

The race was Imola 2009, Marco had been asked to stand in for Nakano who was injured. I went to Mugello and saw that he had adapted to the new bike very quickly. I already followed Superbike for La7 television and the morning of the race I said to him: 'Look, if you make a good start to the race I'm going to have fun commentating!' But in race 1 he started badly. Not slightly badly, but really badly. Then he began to make a great recovery, great pace, until he crashed. OK, one down. They prepared for race 2. I sent a message via a colleague to Marco: 'Great start earlier, you were like a lamppost!' The colleague didn't understand the sense and was a bit embarrassed; he wasn't so confident around Marco, who'd already won the 250 title and so on. 'Go and tell him this from me, no worries,' I said. And he did it. In race 2 we had a lot of fun: firstly because Marco passed Ben Spies and above all because he then passed Max Biaggi. And the funny thing is that Aligi had warned him: 'Don't do anything stupid like overtake Biaggi!' So at the end of the race, as he got off the bike, he made a comment that went down in history:

'OH, WE DID SOMETHING STUPID!'

Marco finished third but that podium was almost like a GP race win. And in Italy, at Imola... The crowds on track for the podium ceremony were all there for him. And the great thing was that he was still on course to take the 250 title, he still had the final rush of his season ahead of him.

At Valencia, the final race of the year, I was at the long turn, the last one after the finish line. Out of superstition I was holding a white T-shirt that I'd taken without saying anything to anybody, and a marker pen. If there was going to be a great last minute surprise, we had at least one shirt to celebrate with! We would have done it, no problem! When Aoyama exited the straight I'd already taken the cap off the pen! But nothing doing, it obviously wasn't meant to be Marco's title...

If there was one thing he wasn't lacking, it was courage – he'd always throw himself into the corners. A way of riding that he'd carried all the way through from minibike racing – Marco weighed 20 kilos more than the others and through the turns he needed to be aggressive because if he wasn't, they'd screw him on the straight and then he'd have to catch up. This style stayed with him, and it was what made him great, because taking the perfect line is all well and good, as is having race pace, whatever you want... But in the end, if you watch a race, what you want to see is the pass.

> **"IT'S IMPOSSIBLE TO BREATHE EASY IF YOU WANT TO STAY UP FRONT. "**

RAFFAELE DE ROSA

PHILLIP ISLAND

THE BEST PHOTO WITH MARCO IS AT PHILLIP ISLAND. WE'RE ON THE PODIUM TOGETHER AND HE'S LIFTING ME UP IN HIS ARMS.

SUPERBIKE

PAOLO One day in 2009 we got a call from Giampiero Sacchi who was looking for Marco and asked him: 'You fancy coming to Imola on Sunday?'

'No, sorry, I'm busy, I can't, I want to stay quiet.'

'No, you don't understand,' he said, 'Nakano is injured, do you want to come and ride the factory Aprilia RSV4 for this Superbike race?'

'I would say yes straight away, but I should speak to Aligi...'

After talking with Aligi, and considering the risks and the pros and cons, we decided to go. 'I'll come and race at Imola but you have to give me the 250 bike.' Of course he wanted the RSA, the latest evolution that they'd given him from Sachsenring onwards, not the less competitive one that he'd used during the first half of the season, the LA that Aligi now looks after at his house. This was the contract that he made with Aprilia, a verbal contract, and they were really great and kept their promise.

He needed to try this Superbike, a four-stroke 1000 derived from the production bike, much heavier and more physically challenging than the two-stroke Grand Prix bikes he'd ridden up until then. So one afternoon we went to Mugello to test it. Marco brought Aligi with him of course and found a completely new team there, with experience of this bike, so Aligi played the part of the guru. Marco rode and in the end he recorded a time that was one-tenth of a second quicker than Max Biaggi. So at 6pm, once the red light was on and the track closed, Biaggi went out to do one last lap, he didn't want to have to say that Simoncelli had gone faster than him. He managed to go a few thousandths quicker than Marco but in the meantime press releases had already gone out...

Marco immediately liked the Superbike, but he didn't yet know the MotoGP and this gave him a bit of extra confidence. Later he told me why: 'Shit, if I ride the Superbike like this, I'll have a field day with the MotoGP.'

With a day's testing under his belt we went to Imola and started practice. The track had been resurfaced and there were issues, it was ridiculously slippery. The riders stopped because the asphalt was no good, there was no grip, while Marco continued to lap, he didn't give a shit... They had to stop him, he was the only one on track, and I remember that Brazzi was there – he lives in Imola and had come to visit us in the pits. He'd followed Marco's success in 250 and every so often if he saw him he'd say: 'Bravo Marco, you deserve it.' At the end of the day Brazzi had behaved really badly in 2006, but the real damage was done by the team, when he got sick and there was no technical direction anymore. Someone told me that when they asked him: 'But why was it that you didn't understand Marco?' he said: 'I've never seen a rider improve so quickly.' For him it was impossible that this '80-kilo donkey' could have become so fast in such a short time.

During practice Simoncelli was impressed by Fabrizio who passed him with the Ducati as soon as he got on track. Because in 250 the Dunlop tyres would throw you off if they weren't up to temperature while the Pirellis in Superbike don't need to be warmed up, they're ready almost immediately. This was another thing he learned – a different way of racing with new tyres.

In free practice, before qualifying and Superpole, he'd crashed at the Tosa turn with the bike that he felt more comfortable on. The other bike was not exactly the same, we don't know why, but sometimes it happens that two identical bikes have different characters.

With the second bike he couldn't ride as well, but he did it anyway and got into the top eight that would fight for Superpole. I remember the applause and the elation of the crowd. At that point he wanted to get on the front row but it wasn't possible because in the confusion of sorting out the bike he'd crashed with, someone forgot to check the oil level, to top it up. So Marco passed in front of the pits, ready to start his flying lap. We saw that his time at the first split was again one second from the fastest and we wondered if he'd gone long again. But instead, as he was braking at the S before Tamburello, the engine went into safety mode, because inertia was moving the oil forwards, and the sensors, sensing the lack of oil, protected the engine by switching it off. In the end he stopped and said: 'But this bike... the red light comes on and it short circuits!!' This is why he ended up eighth.

On the day of the race he was relaxed because he liked the bike and the more he rode, the more he liked it, everything was going well. He started, at one point he overtook many guys but then, setting his sights on the three leaders, he crashed at Tosa. Knowing that he had to do another race he was careful to not get wound up, and he came back calm, the only problem was his leathers – he had to start with a damaged set because he'd crashed and he didn't have a spare set.

He made a better start in the second race, just a bit caught up in traffic but he started passing everyone, at Rivazza he passed Spies on the inside, you didn't see much on TV but it was amazing. Then he went after Biaggi, his team-mate, who was third and had let Haga and Fabrizio pull away on their Ducatis – they would fight it out for first. It looked like Max Biaggi had problems, because he allowed himself to be caught. Marco with some hard braking got past him through the Variante Basso in what I think was a brilliant move. When he passed him, Biaggi wasn't having it, he started riding with more aggression and in the last eight, ten laps he did everything to try and take Marco.

One thing I liked about that day was that when I was in the grandstand watching the race, a lady came up to me and said: 'Tell your son that all the crowds are here for him.' And it was true that when he passed there was a roar as if it were Agostini in his golden days... That evening I told him: 'Marco, today was the equivalent of a World Championship.'

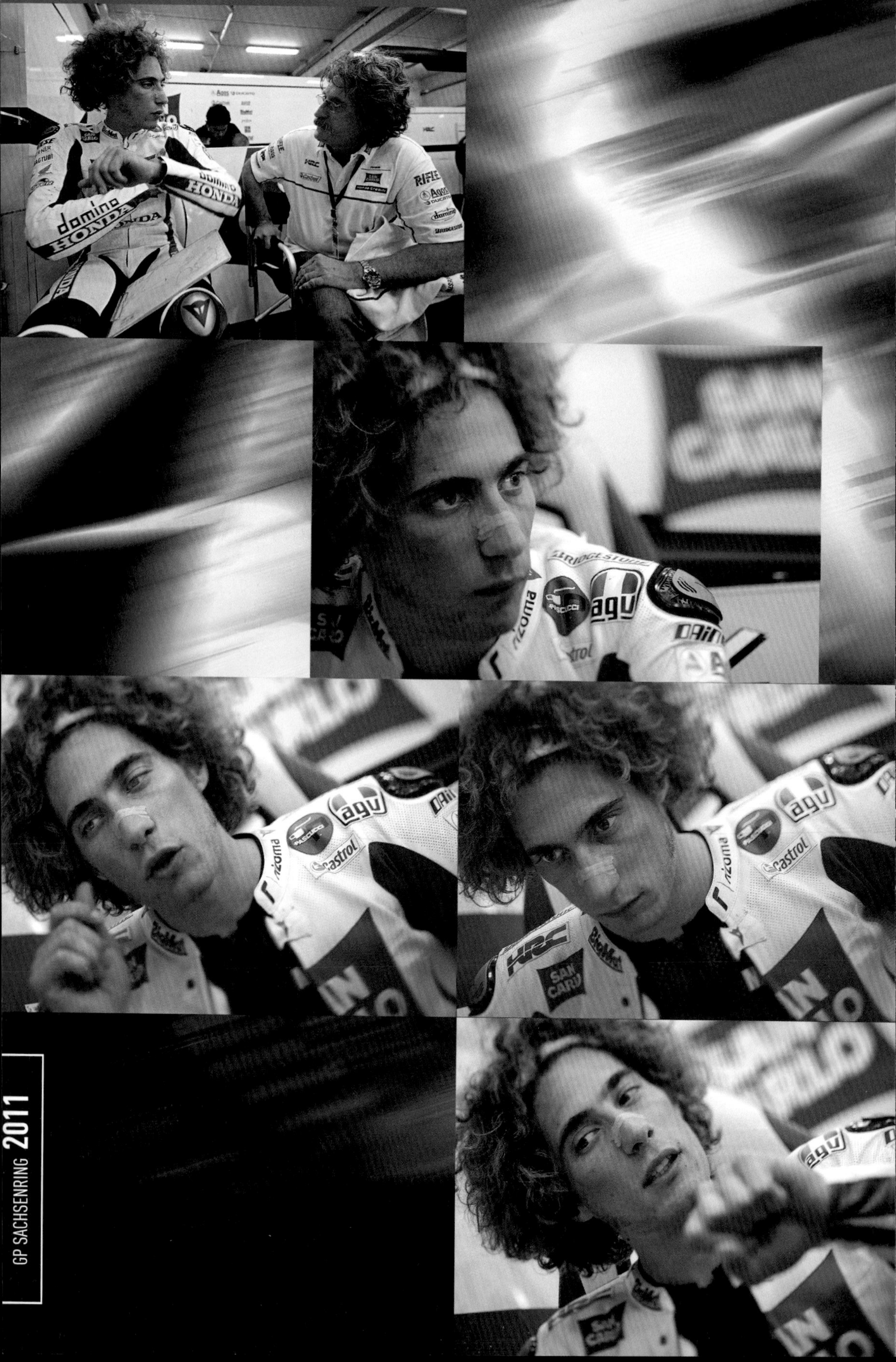

GP SACHSENRING 2011

MARCO WAS THE NEW UP AND COMING ITALIAN RIDER, ACTUALLY HE'D ALREADY ARRIVED. THIS YEAR HE WOULD HAVE THRASHED THEM ALL.

" I'VE DREAMED OF GETTING TO 500,
TO MOTOGP, SINCE I WAS LITTLE. "

AT THE MARKET

PAOLO In 2008, after his win, we had our first dealings with MotoGP – Poncharal contacted us in Assen with regard to Yamaha. It had always been clear that Poncharal thought highly of Marco, you could feel it in his words, his greetings and his hugs and it almost seemed logical to me that the first MotoGP meeting would be organised by him. I remember the first time that he saw him race in 2002 in Brazil, at Jacarepaguá. Even though Marco finished a bit behind, he'd stopped him and told him: 'You'll become a great MotoGP rider.'

That day at Assen we'd fixed a meeting in our camper. Poncharal arrived with Lin Jarvis, the European boss of Yamaha's racing activity, he sat down and started by talking about our camper: 'Small but really nice', then he said, 'We have Valentino Rossi and Lorenzo for now. I'm asking you to come and race with us because the future for us is you and Lorenzo.' It was a great sentence and all of the conditions were right. When they left Marco and I hugged, not because we'd closed the deal, but out of satisfaction that Yamaha had come to us. But Marco wanted to do another year in 250: 'Dad, I worked so hard to get here, now that I really feel at ease on the bike I want to do another year as World Champion.'

Colaninno, president of the Piaggio group, had meanwhile decided that Marco should stay with Aprilia, or Gilera to be exact, though the bike only differed in brand name. We learned that, in a meeting, Colaninno had told his managers: 'You can do as you like but Simoncelli is racing with us.' He'd left them little room to manoeuvre and Marco was proud of it because the two of them had a great relationship and would speak informally to each other. I remember one call: 'Ciao President, how are you?', while many others would bow down and crawl on the floor... After the World Championship we were at a Piaggio convention at Montecarlo and Sacchi, wanting to talk about Marco, told Colaninno, who was there on the front row: 'But President, in Malaysia he cost us 3,000 euro in fines because he did a lap without his helmet.' I remember Colaninno's reply very well: 'And it was worth it!'

In 2009 MotoGP negotiation started again in earnest. We met with the Yamaha managers again at Assen, Poncharal was there again, but this time we went to their motorhome. They wouldn't allow us to bring our technicians because they said that MotoGP is challenging, with very complicated electronics and Poncharal had his own team while the Japanese took care of the electronics.

But Aldo Drudi knew Fausto Gresini and I believe he asked him: 'Why don't you take him?' After the Le Mans Grand Prix where Marco won a great race in the wet, an email quickly arrived from Honda in Japan, asking for a meeting with Simoncelli on the Thursday of the Mugello Grand Prix weekend, in their hotel near Bologna airport, and telling us not to tell anyone. The meeting was fixed for 9.30am, we exited the gate at Mugello at 8.30am, as everyone was coming in... We looked at each other and said: 'OK, let's go on a mission!' Strangely enough we got to the hotel on time and as soon as we crossed the threshold the Japanese interpreter came out to welcome us. At that point Marco said: 'Excuse me, is there a bathroom?' And so we ended up late... Out of the bathroom, it must have been 9.40am, we went downstairs to a private meeting room and found ourselves in front of Ishii, Nakamoto and the interpreter. It was really a secret meeting and the first thing that struck me was the fact that they bowed to us and put their business cards in front of us. While they each pulled out business cards Marco and I looked at each other: all Marco had done was note down what we wanted to ask on a scrap of paper torn from an exercise book...

The best thing about this meeting was the speed of it. I'll never forget it. 9.40am: 'Good morning.' Nakamoto started, saying; 'Right, we're thinking that you could be our factory rider next year and we'd put you in Team Gresini. What do you think?' Marco replied: 'Good, I'm happy, I'd be pleased to. But I am taller than the others and I need different things: will you make all those changes for me?' Nakamoto's terse reply: 'You are a factory rider.' Then Marco asked him: 'I know myself and I need some time, then once I get there I'm fast, so I'd like a two or three year contract.' 'Ok, no problem.' Marco: 'I'd like to bring my crew chief and two mechanics with me because they're my team, I get on with them.' 'No problem.' At that point Marco stood and pulled that crumpled bit of paper from his pocket: 'OK, so I've said that, I've said that...' There was nothing more to say. Nakamoto said: 'So everything's sorted, we'll sign the contract. How much do you want?' Wow! To tell the truth we knew exactly what to ask for but it didn't seem very polite. Marco, intelligently, said: 'I'll think about it and I'll tell you on Sunday at Mugello. But everything's fine with us, we can sign.' These were his words. So at a quarter to ten we were in the car park outside the hotel, hugging – for us it was a done deal. The rapport between Marco and Nakamoto was immediate, you could tell they wanted us, they appreciated Marco and had even complimented him on the race prior to Le Mans. Marco would melt when these things happened...

At that point we needed to set a salary. That Sunday at 7pm, after the Mugello race, we found ourselves in Gresini's motorhome: Nakamoto, Ishii, Marco and me. Sitting to one side there was also Gresini and Pernat. Marco and Nakamoto did it all, as if they were at the market. It was great: 'So how much do you want?' Marco started by saying two million. Nakamoto replied: 'Come on, let's say 1.5 in the first year and we see how you go.' At that point I said: 'Marco, go with 1.8 for each year, it's a good deal.' They looked at each other and said, 'OK', and he and Nakamoto gave each other a high five. All done; in ten minutes they'd made a contract. That was one of the best days of Marco's career. He was proud, he'd got a great contract, both economically speaking and as far as technical conditions were concerned – two years and the option for a third. The adventure began there. He was officially a Honda HRC rider.

Grazie per un Sogno Marco   MARCO lives foerer in our herts

Presi a grande aspettazione   Masanori. Takahashi

Ciao Super Sic

ou will always
in our hearts.
r peace
Super Sic
Shinobu Sato

R.I.P SUPER Sic!
TDVB

R.I.P. MARCO!
TETSUO. SUZUKI

Rest Marco's soul. We LOVE Marco!

Thank you for your riding!   Thank you!!
TN

R.I.P

Ciao Marco!
Noi non da dimenticheremo
Noi e Pa.

to You my
ondolences
Nobuo Ono

Thank you
"Super SIC!
Please rest in peace
Soul!

I'm very sad.
I like your aggressive
riding.
Thank you MARCO.
Taka

R.I.P Marco.

Marco,
L'anima grand
vivra sempre

I wont forget you forever.

Honda

感動をありがとう！！！

The MotoGP dream

ありがとうございました!!
お休み下さい… 今里

ご冥福をお祈りいたします。
梅田

感動をありがとう！

"MY TEAM IS MAINLY ITALIAN BUT AS THERE ARE MANY JAPANESE FROM HONDA, WE ALL SPEAK IN ENGLISH. IT'S LUCKY BECAUSE WE SPEAK IT BADLY BUT THE JAPANESE ALSO SPEAK IT BADLY, SO WE UNDERSTAND EACH OTHER. "

The first time that I went to meet the Simoncelli family, Marco came to meet me at the exit to Riccione and said: 'Hey, get in with me.' We didn't know each other very well and I remember that at the first roundabout he went around twice because he wanted to drift and impress me. We got to his house and they were all sitting around that big table. I remember that Aldo Drudi was there too and Marco started asking me a ton of questions, it was like he was studying me, as if he wanted to understand how I was inside. And I immediately saw the devotion and consideration that Marco's parents had for him. It was always a unique relationship, especially with his dad, and he was always proud of this.

In 2009 I started to speak to Marco about MotoGP. I told him: 'Look, Honda is interested; they want to meet you...' And him: 'They want to meet me? They know me?' He almost seemed shocked... I had fixed a meeting with Nakamoto in a hotel in Bologna and I remember that after the meeting Marco said to me: 'Ah, easy, nice, in five minutes we fixed everything, we're already set.' Then I remember we had a second meeting there at Mugello to talk about budgets.

MARCO AND NAKAMOTO WERE A BIT LIKE TWO NEAPOLITANS PLAYING A GAME OF *BRISCOLA*.

'One year, two years...' Nakamoto undoubtedly had a long-term view and had great trust in this kid that had just arrived.

Marco was always a very special person, valour was very important to him. He was determined and very loyal, he was transparent. Even in the difficult times Marco was someone who'd say: 'Come on, damn it, we're in the shit but we'll get out of it, I'm telling you.' He knew where he was, he knew what he had to do and how to do it. I remember the first bad crash in Malaysia with the MotoGP, an hour later he was calm: 'Come on, let's go and see the others riding...'

HE WASN'T SOMEONE WHO'D GET SCARED, HE WAS A GLADIATOR AND HE'D FIGHT WITH THE ENTHUSIASM OF ONE WHO WAS ENJOYING HIMSELF.

It was great because Marco believed and would always question himself, he was a warrior, one who'd never give up. Even when there were difficult times, like when he received the threats – at first he was shocked but then he relaxed and said: 'And what of it? What are they going to do to me?' The police escorts became his number one fans, they would have defended him anyway.

I learned many things from Marco. His behaviour was exemplary: his way of living, his way of being made him a really special person. You don't meet people like that. I've not met any others. He was all good, damn it. Marco never made me angry, maybe he didn't want to go and do something for a sponsor and he'd say: 'Oh do I really have to do it?'

'Marco you have to do it.' And he'd go: 'Oh OK, if I have to do it then I'll do it.' This was the most he'd say. He was a professional, he never left anything to chance. To look at him he might have seemed like an easy-going kid but he was in fact meticulous. Then in the evening he'd play cards with his dad and with his mechanics, he'd joke around, he lived a relaxed lifestyle, he'd have fun, get friends together. It was nice precisely because you didn't feel that you were at a Grand Prix, Marco was there and he was fine, that was his life, the most beautiful thing in the world. He felt part of a family with a loyal spirit and had a group of people around him that he liked.

In Malaysia he'd suffer with the heat and I remember that after the first year, when we went testing Paolo had brought him a paddling pool full of ice, but when he put him in it he couldn't hold him because he'd do everything to escape. It was freezing! Marco told me afterwards: 'My dad is still strong... I tried to escape and he held me there. I couldn't do it... but afterwards I felt better can you believe it?'

CARLO MERLINI	TAKE IT OR LEAVE IT

It was 2010 and we were in Qatar for a very important race: Marco's first official MotoGP. Finally the championship that counted.

    I don't know how excited or emotional he was. I only know that, when we sat down for lunch in hospitality, he found himself next to the president of San Carlo, Alberto Vitaloni. Marco had maybe only seen him once, they'd never even shaken hands I don't think... OK, anyway, we can say they barely knew each other!

    And so what does Marco do? He looks at him, smiles and says: 'Alberto, what hotel are you staying in?'

    'Alberto???' Everyone called him president...

    'I'm at the Four Seasons', replied Vitaloni. 'Why?'

    'Oh lord, the hooker hotel!'

    There, I knew it. The blood froze in my veins. Unbelievable. Can you believe that someone would be so confident in front of the president of the main sponsor?

    But that's where Marco would get you. I expected the president to give him a dirty look at that point, or a tight smile, to avoid an argument. But no. In fact it was precisely his straightforwardness that led to their complicity. Vitaloni looked at him and smiled. I continued to think: 'OK, now he's going to blow', but instead he smiled.

    But I know why:

MARCO WOULD WIN YOU OVER WITH THAT STUFF, PRECISELY BECAUSE HE WAS WITHOUT FRILLS, UNPREDICTABLE. TAKE IT OR LEAVE IT.

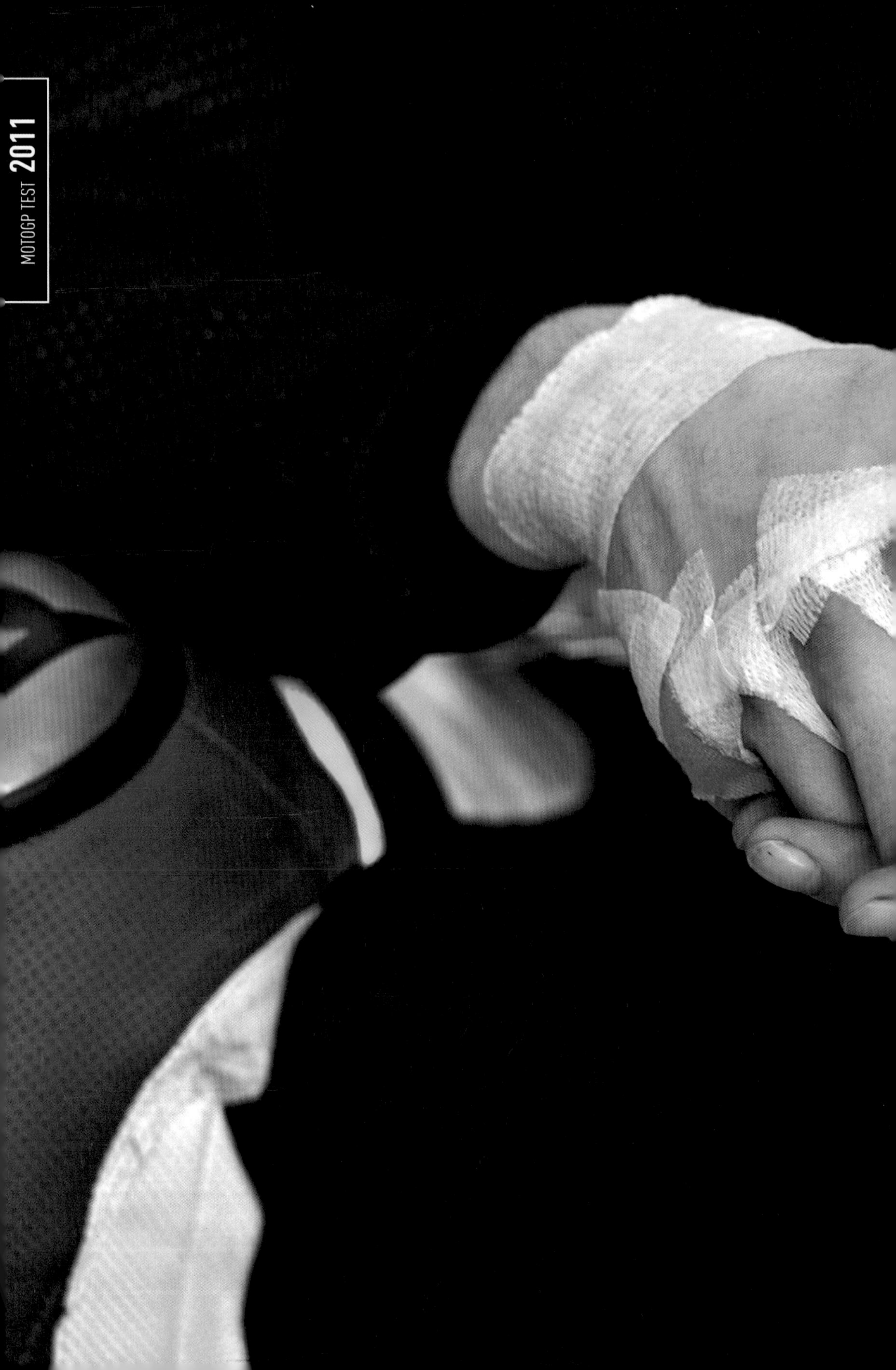

TESTING

PAOLO At the end of 2009, as well as the new ruling that meant we couldn't move to the factory team, they also cancelled a lot of tests due to the economic crisis. Riders that had moved to MotoGP earlier had 80,000km of testing over the winter and countless tyres available, so they'd ride all winter. In terms of kilometres winter testing was the equivalent of all of the seasons' GPs combined.

But that year the rookies were only allowed to do three days of testing before Christmas, they'd even cut an hour of Friday morning practice time during the Grand Prix... Those bikes are perfect, engineering masterpieces and if you can't test them, set them up, racing becomes really difficult. Marco was also at a big disadvantage because he was taller and heavier than the others and had to be on a bike made for a little guy like Pedrosa. Marco was someone who needed time to get there and in that first year in MotoGP we were really faced with a difficult task.

I remember that, during the first tests in Malaysia, in trying to stay with Hayden he suffered a massive highside... he lost the front, he was used to the 250 and tried to hold it with his knee but when the rear wheel regained traction it launched him into the air like a catapult, if he'd just let it go maybe it wouldn't have happened. It was Marco's first big crash, they had to take him to hospital. He hadn't broken anything, but he couldn't remember anything.

We arrived in Kuala Lumpur after about 20 minutes. They looked at him in the ER and then, having established it was nothing serious, they put him in a room. Me, Elvio and another mechanic were in the waiting room. At a certain point I saw Elvio get really pale and he passed out, because you only have to mention blood and he gets ill. We took him, put his legs up... The funny thing was that we had one there in the wars and this one here passing out, the only one of us who spoke English...

A couple of hours passed and finally I was able to speak with Marco, he looked pretty good but he still couldn't remember anything. So I told him: 'Marco, I don't know, maybe we've made a mistake? Maybe we really need a team that knows the bike...' And his memory came back, just like that! It was amazing, I'll remember it for as long as I live. Just as I mentioned his team his memory returned: 'I remember now dad. This, this and this happened.' He gave me a blow-by-blow account of the accident, then we went back but he didn't go to rest, no, we went trackside, in the car with Gresini, to watch the other riders. He spent all afternoon there, going from turn to turn to see what was happening.

WHERE ARE WE GOING TO EAT?

ROSSELLA Marco lost his memory on another occasion too, as a child. He was at the sea with my cousin and her two children, Riccardo and Daniele. I went to collect them at around seven in the evening, because I had to go to work, and I took them to eat at my mum's.

En route Marco asked: 'Where are we going to eat this evening?'

'At grandma's.'

Then he repeated the question three, four, five times, continuously and in the end I asked him a bit angrily: 'What did you do, did you bang your head?'

And Daniele said in a little voice: 'Yes, Auntie, he banged his head'.

'But how?'

'Um, he fell from the slide, he hit his head. Then a man took him and put him under the cold shower and he was a bit better...'

So it had happened at about three or four in the afternoon and then Marco had stayed in the sun until seven, having hit his head like that and now he couldn't remember anything.

I said: 'Why didn't you kids tell your mum?'

'Um, because we were scared she'd yell at us.'

I took Marco, we went straight to the ER in Rimini and they kept him under observation for three days because he really couldn't remember a thing. Then bit by bit, with our help, his memory came back.

A QUESTION OF TIME

PAOLO For us MotoGP got off to a very difficult start, it was a question of time for both him and the team. The 250 had less electronics; it was more about human power while the MotoGP had this technical perfection...

Marco had wanted his team, but we quickly realised that the MotoGP was perfection: a very sophisticated machine where you can set the bike up for every metre of the track, but it's you that has to feel it, manage it and understand it. Courage isn't enough; you need thick skin, class and technique. You have to fine tune it, the electronics are incredible and allow you to go fast, but compared to the 250 it's a totally different thing and the whole team had to fight along with Marco to get there.

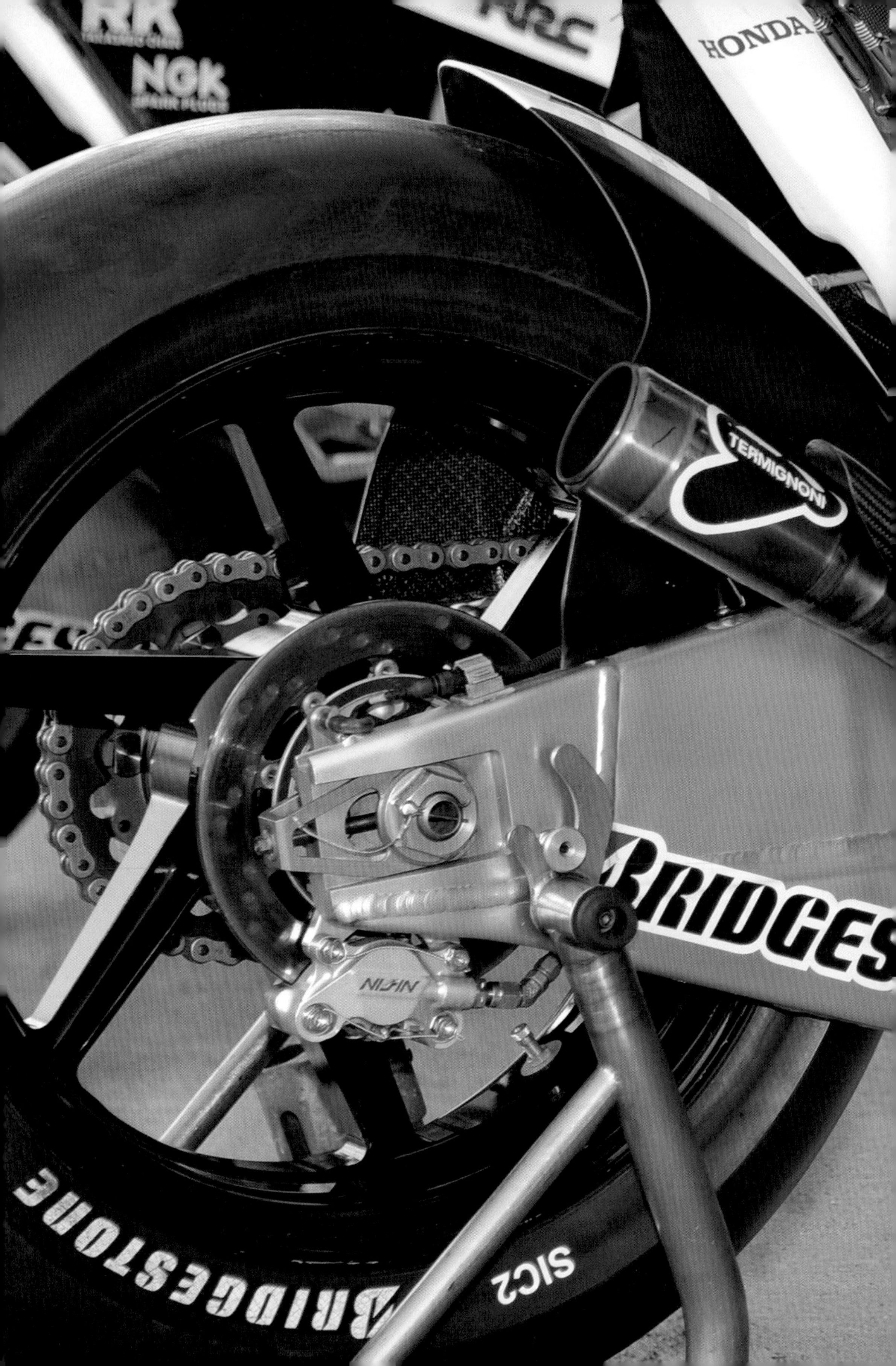
RK
NGK
HONDA
TERMIGNONI
BRIDGES
BRIDGESTONE
SIC2

The one who made an impressive step up, something that was really needed, was Elvio. At the start they questioned him and even for Marco, who'd always stick up for his guys, it was a really complicated situation. Now he's one of the best telemetry guys in MotoGP, in the end he did all the mapping, down to the last detail.

In the meantime Marco had grown too, and Aligi along with them. They began to understand everything and really became difficult to beat, they were fantastic.

When there were difficulties, in that first year, Aligi and Marco would go to Sardinia to relax. Marco would say he was going to the sea with grandpa and grandma: 'But what a great place to be, look how beautiful it is!' It was awesome – with the sea in front of them, on that beach, the two of them would find the serenity and strength with which to continue the following week.

I'M GOING TO THE BEACH WITH MY GRANDPARENTS

ROSSELLA Aligi gave Marco a lot and taught him so much, including how to save energy instead of getting angry, which isn't constructive. Aligi taught him to concentrate instead on things in which he could improve. Their connection was wonderful and Rita, his wife, always said that Marco also taught Aligi many things. Marco had huge respect and love for him, because he was someone who was able to really care about many people without taking anything away from anybody. The more there were of them, the most love he had to give, it was his prerogative.

> " I OWE EVERYTHING TO MY PARENTS. IF THEY HADN'T ENCOURAGED AND SUPPORTED ME, I WOULDN'T HAVE GOT TO WHERE I AM NOW.
> THEN LUCKILY I FOUND THIS CREW CHIEF, ALIGI DEGANELLO – HE'S REALLY GREAT, BOTH ON A TECHNICAL AND HUMAN LEVEL. WHEN YOU'RE IN THE GARAGE I THINK IT'S REALLY IMPORTANT TO FEEL THAT THEY TRUST YOU AND TO KNOW THAT EVEN IF YOU MAKE A MISTAKE NO-ONE WILL POINT THE FINGER. THE IMPORTANT THING IS TO TRY AND SOLVE PROBLEMS AND IMPROVE AS A GROUP, TOGETHER. "

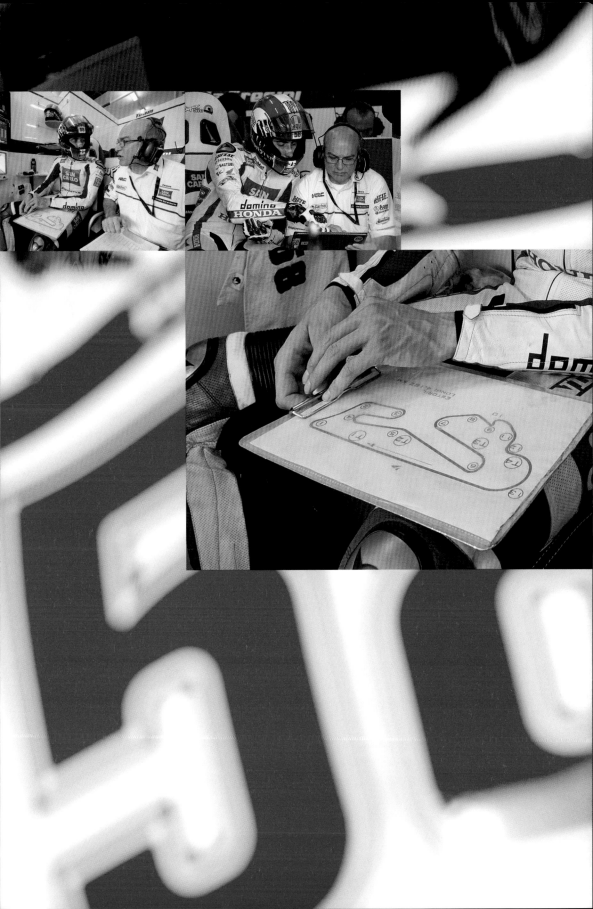

Paolo and Marco went to Fiorenzo Caponera, the owner of team Bravo, and told him: 'We want Aligi as crew chief.' I think that someone had suggested it to them, but I was with Steve Jenkner that year and I couldn't leave him for a young kid. Bronzina was working with me so we put together a team for Marco, the new recruit. New young rider, new technician, I gave Bronzina a hand, especially at the start, so I followed Marco indirectly. I remember when we decided to go to Corcovado Mountain, to see Christ the Redeemer, in Brazil. Almost the entire team was there, including Bronzina and the technicians, and we went to take photos at the statue of Christ. But no-one was really interested and in the end there was just me, Paolo and Marco. We took two pictures because in the first my hair caused a glare... I kept one and Paolo kept the other. In 2007, when I returned to work with Marco, Paolo pulled it out: 'Look, this was a sign, the three of us were there then and now we're back together.'

Marco was very critical. I always told him: 'You need to listen to everyone, but not everyone will be right.' Listen to everyone, from the young boy to the old man, the good, the bad, treasure all of it. Someone tells you something stupid, but this too is a treasure and you should take the good from it, or at least that which you consider to be good. As well as listening and being attentive, as well as always having his antennae tuned in, Marco was also able to put things into practice.

IF SOMEONE SAYS TO ME: 'THAT TURN THERE, INSTEAD OF TAKING IT IN SECOND YOU CAN DO IT IN THIRD' I LISTEN BUT MAYBE I WON'T MANAGE TO DO IT IN THIRD, WHILE HE WOULD GO OUT AND DO IT IN THIRD, MAYBE EVEN TRYING FOURTH!

A truly incredible thing. As a result many thought that when he moved from 125 to 250 he'd immediately be fast but, on the contrary, the fact that he was so critical meant that he needed time, he had to think things over. He'd work at it and he'd get there. Because he had great talent and wasn't one of those 'make it or break it' guys, even if it might have looked like it from the outside. In reality he was very attentive to the set-up of his bike, to its construction from the point of view of both a person and a rider.

I got on very well with Marco because there was sharing between us, I would give him things and he would give me things. I'm quite introverted, perhaps out of shyness, and he was the complete opposite, extroverted, bringing people together, he liked to be in contact with people. He trusted everyone and, actually, over the course of time he had to rethink certain things. Marco was someone who would stay up late to be with his friends, he was never tired, while I always have trouble with these things. But I soon saw that he would make us do things, like in Sardinia when we'd always go somewhere or go karting, simple things but we'd have so much fun. It was then that I realised that perhaps you needed to make a little effort to be able to do wonderful things with others.

It was this constant sharing that was so great with Marco. We were so involved that when it came to certain things we would understand each other immediately, perhaps with a glance. Marco would realise that something was not right by my change in attitude and vice versa, this was really nice. But these are things that happen over time and by spending time together, with that pragmatism. I was able to understand when he was down because if we were there talking and he would look away it meant that something had happened. Marco was extremely transparent – maybe at times there are things you can't say, you don't show them because they've told you not to but he couldn't do it, he'd really struggle. I'm similar, I find it hard to lie and so we went hand in hand.

MARCO ALWAYS WANTED TO WIN, AT ALL COSTS.

I remember once in Sardinia, we went karting and everyone was there: me, my son Elvin, Marco, Kate, our Sardinian friends and the guy renting the karts. Marco set off, shoving everyone like there was no tomorrow, Kate was in front because she's lighter and so had managed to take the lead. We got to the first turn, he was already passing her but seeing as she was there he shoved her anyway... He won easily and at the end of the race I asked him: 'Lord, did you really need to shove her like that?' 'Well she was there, it was fun, I gave her a big shove!' 'But when you saw that we'd all stopped you could have slowed down, we'd have restarted,' I said. 'Um, you know, I thought about it but I was scared of finishing second!' he replied. His desire to win even the unimportant things was sheer fun, like when we played marbles on the sand, some incredible arguments! 'No, you pushed it!' He was wonderful.

In Malaysia perhaps he was a little too daring in trying to stay with the leaders. He was battling with Bautista, went a little long and crashed, resulting in him coming back to the garage angry and upset...

Before that race he'd been on the podium in Australia and after Sepang we'd go to Valencia, another track where he was already really fast in 2010.

In the winter tests in Malaysia Marco had been quick, lapping with similar times to Lorenzo, Stoner and Pedrosa. In the race we wanted to win, aware that Marco was fast on this track, aware that he had grown. But during the practices we saw that things had changed – the lap times were not like those recorded in testing and, very probably, the others were a little more sorted than us. We could run a good race, maybe reach the podium, but winning it... I should have told him: 'Look Marco, the others are in a better position, with the times we've done we're not where we were in February. We need to just try and do a good race and then we'll go to Valencia.' I'm really sorry that I didn't try to curb his certainty about winning. I regret not having done anything to reduce the pressure a bit.

Marco was incredibly at ease around people, he was very natural, even with disabled people, extraordinary. It was because he trusted everyone and had spontaneity... I appreciated this and, on one side, I also envied him, it was one of those things I tried to copy. When you see someone having difficulty you're worried about bothering them, you don't know what to do, 'do I look, not look, touch, not touch' but he was totally self-assured, really capable. This is why I think that one day he would have done something important, beyond motorcycling. Marco was a generous person, 100 per cent, fair with everyone, special in his normality, his naturalness and his ability to love everyone. He wasn't a hero but a very rare creature nowadays. He believed that everyone should be his friend and vice versa. So much so that perhaps he suffered more than others when someone would block him, as several riders did over the years, or when he was reproached. He'd get upset. When they threatened him he suffered deeply: 'But why, what have I done wrong? I'm nice to everyone, why would someone have a problem with me?' He was a delightful person from that point of view, truly rare.

HE WAS HAPPY. HE KNEW HE WAS LIVING WELL, THAT HE HAD A GREAT FAMILY. HE WAS AWARE THAT HE WAS ENJOYING HIMSELF AND HE SAVOURED THE SMALL THINGS.

Thinking back to the 125 races he'd say to me: 'Heck, if I'd had the head that I have now I'd have thrown away a lot less races', because in 125 when he saw someone ahead of him, through a turn where maybe you couldn't go any quicker than that guy was going, he'd go full throttle to catch him and would, of course, finish on the grass. He'd give it his all, he'd do things regardless, as he did with people, he trusted everyone... Compared to other riders that would reflect more, this was a defect of his, to such an extent that in 2007 I gave him some homework. 'Take all the risks of any case and then try and weigh it all up. Anything, a bike ride or a wheelie – consider how someone might step out to cross the road'. And he improved a lot. At the end of the year, during the race at Valencia, when there was some kind of contact with Debón who passed him on the straight and went to close the door, Marco wanted to resist but the other guy forced him out. He went on to the gravel but stayed upright, returning to the track twelfth or thirteenth and lapping with similar times to the leaders. But these are things that only the guy recording the times sees.

When he railroaded me and the other guys into moving to Honda, I hope it was a considered decision. Because you can keep a friendship and say: 'Look, I'm going to a team where they already have everything I need.' You stay friends, you see each other, you go and eat pizza, nothing changes. But he had been burned in 250, where he should have gone to the factory team, the best of the best, but it didn't happen. So when he went to MotoGP, he didn't want to leave a team where we all understood each other perfectly, where each of us fully trusted the other. I trusted him totally, because we could always talk about things, and he probably trusted me.

I was the first to say: 'Look, if we have to stay together just because we get along, we're going to do serious things here, so let's try...' But he told me: 'No, no, I want you, I want the team.' Me, Elvio and Maciste were the only ones to go in the end, he couldn't take everyone because Gresini had his own team. As well as being invaluable from a human point of view, I think it was also an intelligent move.

For the love of god, perhaps it could have gone even better for him but Marco had, as always, the courage to take risks. If I'd been in his shoes, maybe I'd have done the same. **BECAUSE WHEN YOU'RE WITH SOMEONE THAT YOU TRUST 100 PER CENT, YOU CAN ALSO MAKE A LEAP INTO THE UNKNOWN...**

ELVIO DEGANELLO	A LEAP INTO THE UNKNOWN

One of the things that I loved doing with Marco was re-watching the races together, straight after they'd finished. We'd meet up once we'd dismantled the garage and go to Marco's camper. I would sleep a bit and watch a bit, we'd stop and rewind and then watch it again. And in the end we'd interpret our feelings from the videos into technical information. Most of the time it was easier to solve things by going on Marco's feelings rather than with the telemetry data – it was more immediate, more real.

He was like that, he'd try and try again, he'd capture each detail and work at it until he managed to improve.

ON THE STARTING LINE

PAOLO I think I'm the only dad who went out on the MotoGP starting line. There aren't any other parents but Marco wanted me, because he trusted me and knew that I wouldn't say stupid things.

I would keep quiet, I'd watch what was happening, I'd keep an eye on him but from the sidelines, then at a certain point during the day he'd say: 'So, dad?'

When he'd say 'So, dad?' I had the floor; I could say what I liked and he'd listen, but he knew that if I needed to call him an ass, I'd call him an ass. This is something that he always acknowledged, in fact I remember that he'd wind me up with Aligi and say: 'Oh, Aligi, it might seem like dad's saying stupid things but in the end he's always right. It might seem like he's saying stupid things...'

STICK WITH ME AND I'LL HELP YOU

PAOLO It was only during practice in Qatar that I began to see Marco more in tune with the bike, despite it still being the bike that was taking him for a ride. During the first tests in Malaysia he had found himself in difficulty, he couldn't record fast times. There we really got to know Loris Capirossi, an extraordinary person. He had seen that we were having a few problems during the tests and when we met up that evening after the sessions he said: 'You're a champion Marco, you don't have to worry. Keep calm, it takes time here.' Yes, it takes time but in the meantime everyone looks at you condescendingly – I think a rider suffers like a dog.

That year Capirossi was always there for Marco, he was forever coming to our garage: 'Marco, come behind me. I'm in the garage next to you, when I go out stick with me and I'll help you, at least you'll make a fast lap.' In reality, if you make a lap behind someone faster you may go a bit better but you don't control the bike, while in MotoGP the most important thing is to understand the bike, so doing a lap behind someone doesn't help you much, it only really helps to create newspaper headlines.

The year after Capirossi moved to Pramac and it was his turn to have a lot of trouble. We were in Malaysia again for testing and in the evening Marco went down to the hotel restaurant and told Loris: 'Stick with me and I'll help you.' It was wonderful because he now knew how to ride, he was no longer a kid that followed others. Now it was him who could say: 'Come on, stick behind me.'

There's a secret to Malaysia – the fast laps are made in the morning, in the first session, when the track's cooler. 'So, OK, tomorrow morning I'll go out on track at 10am precisely,' Marco told him. 'Stick with me and we'll leave the garage together.' Marco was great at these things.

The following morning he prepared, everything was ready, and at 10am precisely he got on the bike and they set off. But after two metres he stopped and switched the bike off – he'd forgotten his ear plugs... Capirossi passed by and entered the track. Marco put his plugs in and set off again but having got off the bike he'd lost one or two laps. Capirossi came behind Marco while he was making a slow lap to raise the tyre temperature, then during the second lap he couldn't hear him anymore. He was distracted and returned, worried, to the garage. 'Did he fall?' While making his fast lap Marco's thoughts had gone to Capirossi, because he couldn't hear him behind him and as Marco had a quicker pace at that point he thought: 'The guy must have risked too much and crashed.' This episode conditioned the entire day of practice. Marco was like that.

The last time we laughed a lot with Marco was in Malaysia, when we were winding up Cecco, Fabrizio Cecchini.

Pirro had told us that Cecco had gone to Aoyama, Marco's team-mate and, half in English and half in romagnolo dialect, had told him: *'Quand erraiv, telefon.'*

This was his English!

As soon as he'd said it, we started to take the piss. And Cecco is a bit cranky.

FROM THAT MOMENT ON MARCO WOULD ALWAYS SHOUT TO THE OTHER GARAGE BEFORE PRACTICE: 'FABRI, QUAND ERRAIV, TELEFON!'

Then he'd put his helmet on and go out. Aligi laughed when he told him. We were at the pool, I said to him: 'Aligi, stop it, you've water in your mouth.'

And him: 'But it's making me laugh so hard!' He was laughing to himself.

And then he started laughing even harder because I was watching Bautista playing tennis when Marco arrived and said: 'What the hell are you looking at?' and wham! He whacked me over the head, as a joke, and Aligi said: 'Ah, I've never seen Marco jealous before' and he started laughing again.

'What the hell are you laughing for?' I asked.

'That direct hit was fantastic', Aligi replied.

At the start Marco was pretty superstitious, getting up as much as an hour ahead of time to do a load of stupid things. He'd position the toothpaste facing up, put his flip flops under the bed, then he'd do something strange with his necklaces, he always did it, right up to the end. He said it helped him to concentrate – he'd intertwine them and look at the light reflecting on them. He'd be rapt. Anyway. He never stopped doing that.

One day I turned the toothpaste around. He went out to practice, he did well, he came back and I said: 'Go and look at the toothpaste.'

Because I think that a superstition is a sign of ignorance, I always told him that and I tell his dad the same thing. Paolo is a bit less superstitious now because he realises that all the things he used to do were useless. I mean come on, superstition has no power over destiny.

GP BARCELLONA **2011**

KATE	THE CABINET

A couple of years ago while they were dismantling the garage one Sunday evening, a member of the other team asked him for a hand: 'Come on Sic, push the cabinet.'

From his chair he looked at him and gave some sort of reply. The guy continued to push the cabinet, on one side he was pretending to laugh but on the other no, because the thing was heavy and no-one was helping him. Marco wasn't doing anything, I turned to him and said: 'Marco, give him a hand! Are you worried you'll break a nail?'

'No, but I might hurt myself...'

'Come on, you'll hurt yourself pushing a cabinet out of the garage! Poor guy, he was there pushing it, killing himself, and you didn't lift a finger to help him.'

Five minutes passed, I left, came back and he was there pulling the carpet that covered the garage floor up: 'Marco, what are you doing?'

'Well, shit, you made me feel guilty and so now I'm helping out.'

I couldn't believe it. 'What's that got to do with it? It's one thing to push a cabinet but another to pull the carpet up, that's not your job, stop it!'

But it was useless, he felt guilty.

And who could stop Marco?

269 |

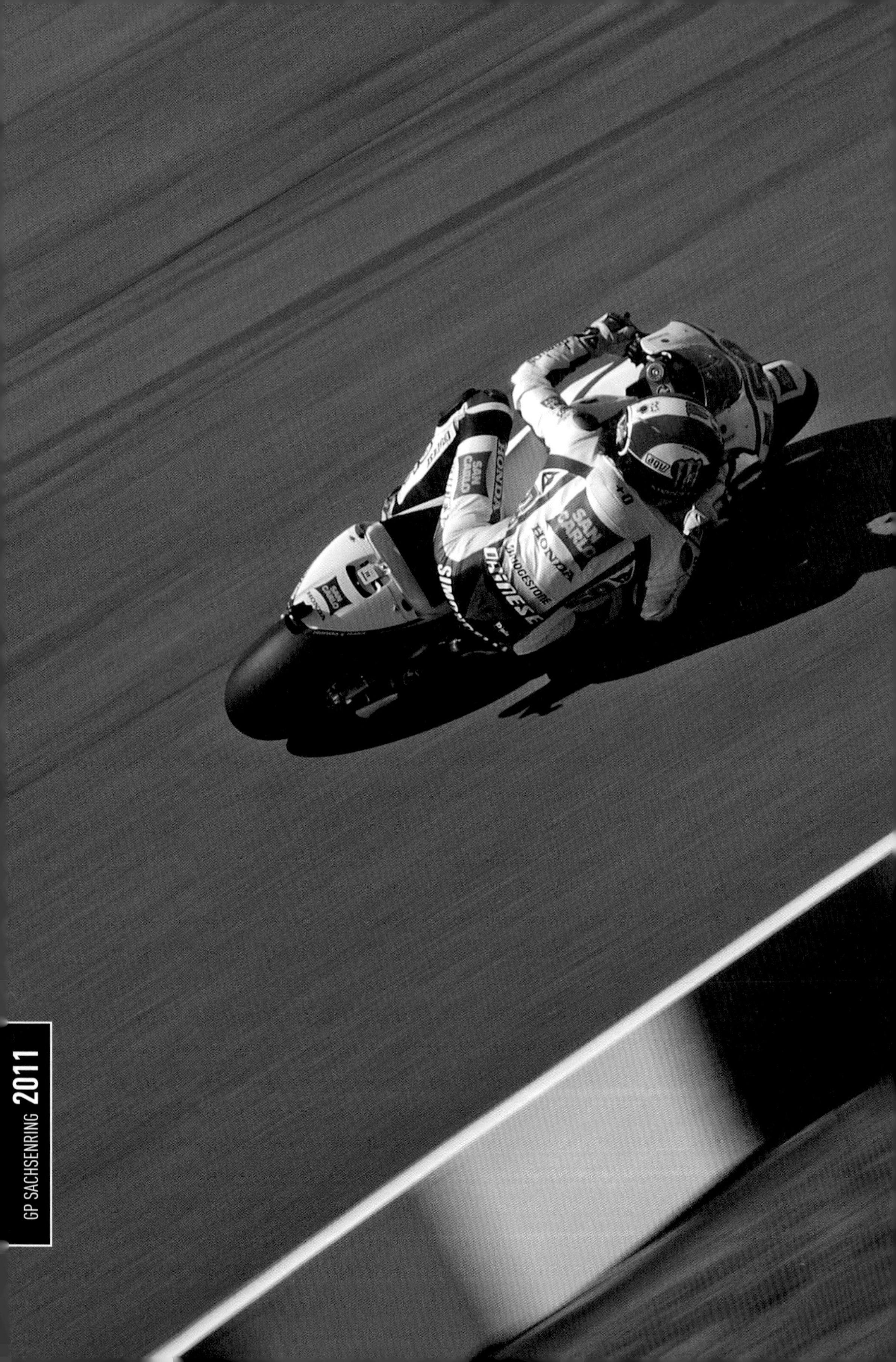
SAN CARLO
HONDA
BRIDGESTONE

"YOU LIVE MORE GOING FULL THROTTLE FOR FIVE MINUTES THAN SOME PEOPLE DO IN A LIFETIME."

THE SEASON STARTS WELL

PAOLO Marco was gradually growing together with the team. Grand Prix after Grand Prix, and in 2011 he'd reached a good level. We were happy, the season was starting well, in fact in February, in the first winter tests in Malaysia, he'd made the fastest lap.

He'd gone well in Qatar, which was one of the toughest tracks for Marco, not because it was difficult per se, but due to consumption, with a limit of 21 litres for the whole race. At that track you keep the throttle open and, weighing 20 kilos more than the others, he had always had consumption problems in the last part of the race, even in 250 and 125. They couldn't give him all the fuel he needed and along the straight he was slower. In qualifying you push as hard as possible, even though you won't be able to in the race. On that occasion, in the final ten minutes, Marco came in one-thousandth of a second behind Lorenzo who was third, so he took the fourth fastest time. I remember how happy Nakamoto was... He went well in the race too, finishing fifth, he ran a great race.

At Jerez it poured down, a soaking wet day. It stopped raining half an hour before the race started. Marco made a good start, made two amazing passes on the wet track, passed Lorenzo with some impressive hard braking through the turn at the end of the straight, precisely where he later crashed. At the end of the other straight he passed Stoner, it was as if they were standing still. So he was leading, he made fifteen laps and he was going great guns, he was already three seconds up on Lorenzo. The problem was those shit tyres – that left their mark on his life – they wouldn't finish the race, and without warning they'd throw you to the ground. A stupid crash, he picked the bike back up, the marshals didn't help him to push, he tried to do it himself, on the slight downhill, but couldn't. He called to them, he wobbled, the bike fell and he folded the handlebar. At that point he exploded in a fit of rage... that day no-one helped him.

After that episode Honda started to take a closer look and they fixed it so that the bike was easier to push start, it only needed a small push. But that crash, that chaotic episode, was necessary. Because, as also happened after his death, they changed the tyres. It's always like that in motorcycling – something has to happen before there is change.

SUPERSIC

PAOLO At Le Mans he took the second fastest time in practice. Marco had now become SuperSic. In the race the track was damp, so he had no problems at the start, he was fourth or fifth, and then he slowly started passing everyone. When he reached Pedrosa he passed him with some hard braking that left Pedrosa looking like an advertising board for Repsol...

He got back past him along the straight but he didn't know Marco well enough. Pedrosa put himself on the inside and Marco went around him. Marco later told me that he thought: 'Do I wait for the next turn or pass him here, going around him and getting the crowd on its feet?' And in those seconds he decided: 'I'll go around and the crowd will get to its feet.' But Pedrosa got scared and instead of continuing to lean and make the turn with Marco he stood the bike back up, made contact, crashed and broke his shoulder. So they gave Marco a ride through penalty and in the end he gave third place away to Valentino Rossi, a dream for him, while he arrived fifth. This was the start of the war between the Spaniards, or Puig's people, and Marco.

"I DON'T FEEL THAT I PLAYED DIRTY. I'M SORRY THAT PEDROSA CRASHED AND HURT HIS COLLARBONE BUT I DON'T THINK I DID ANYTHING WRONG. HE HAD PASSED ME ON THE STRAIGHT, I BRAKED WHERE I USUALLY BRAKE AND I FOUND HIM THROUGH THE TURN BUT I DIDN'T CLOSE, I LEFT HIM ROOM TO ENTER. PEDROSA WENT LONG, I STRAIGHTENED UP AND HE HIT ME. I'M REALLY SORRY FOR DANI, BUT I WAS IN FRONT AND I DIDN'T CLOSE THE DOOR. I LEFT HIM ROOM TO MOVE, THE BIKE BECAME UNSTABLE AND HE FELL. I'M ALSO SORRY ABOUT THE RESULT, TODAY WAS, IN EFFECT, A SECOND PLACE BUT I CAME IN FIFTH, ONLY BECAUSE AFTER THE PENALTY I WAS ABLE TO GET PAST HAYDEN AND SPIES RIGHT AT THE END. IT'S ONE OF THOSE THINGS THAT CAN HAPPEN IN A RACE. ,,

SIC

"MARCO WAS TACTICALLY NAIVE BECAUSE HE WAS FASTER THAN PEDROSA AND COULD HAVE WAITED A MINUTE BEFORE PASSING HIM. INSTEAD HE RISKED TOO MUCH. I'M REALLY HAPPY EVEN IF DOVI HAS BEATEN ME AGAIN. WE STILL HAVE WORK TO DO BUT I'M FINALLY FAST. ,,

VALENTINO ROSSI

" I'M LUCKY... UNLUCKY, I DON'T KNOW, IN THAT MY GIRLFRIEND ALWAYS HOLDS MY UMBRELLA SO WE CAN SAY THAT I DON'T SEE ANOTHER UMBRELLA GIRL'S ARSE, BUT MAYBE, SEEING AS I ALREADY SEE HER ARSE ALL THE TIME, IT MEANS THAT I CONCENTRATE BETTER ON THE RACE. "

LETTERS FROM SPAIN

PAOLO We got home and prepared for Barcelona. One day Fausto Gresini called me and said: 'I need to speak to you, come to Imola, to my office.' I went up and he showed me a letter that he'd received. It said that they would kill Marco in Barcelona, that they'd take him out on the starting line because they'd had enough of him causing others to crash... They also sent a bullet, and used words to really make you shudder. What to do at that point? Firstly we decided to go and report it to the postal police and they immediately started investigating through Interpol while the Italian police together with the Spanish police decided to escort Marco from the moment he arrived at Barcelona airport up until Monday when he'd get back on the plane.

The fun lay in having to tell Marco. 'Do we tell him or not tell him?' and also, 'What shall we do, shall we make this public or not?' In the end we decided that the right thing to do was to make it public and therefore tell Marco. I think this was a winning move because it was too serious a thing. Public opinion, and the Spanish journalists, had to take a step back and lower the volume a bit.

Anyway, someone had to tell Marco, so one evening we were round the table, Aligi and Gresini came, we ate as we usually did and told him. Marco's reaction was: 'But why do they want to kill me? What have I done?' He was upset. But one way or another we managed to calm him and decided to go to the GP, because we could have stayed home and not gone.

But instead we went to the airport and as soon as they opened the plane doors there were two Spanish troopers, Mossos d'Esquadra, two exceptional guys. In one sense it was amazing, it was as if the president of the republic had landed at the airport. We had five people around us, then they put us into two cars and from that moment we weren't left alone even for a moment, not even at night in the camper. Before leaving the garage there was even someone who'd check the high ground with binoculars, it was incredible...

In the end Marco learned to get around with these guys. He continued with his normal life and they followed him when he moved around with the motorino, except that Marco would go too fast and they'd always be a distance behind. In fact Matitaccia, the caricaturist for *Motosprint*, did a cartoon of it, with him in front and two escorts behind shouting: 'Vamos! Vamos!' At the start those two guys were prejudiced but they later understood who Marco was and they became friends.

After his death, they sent me one of the nicest letters that I received. I think that, also on a personal level, it was one of Marco's best weekends, precisely because these guys gradually realised that Marco was nothing like the papers said.

That weekend Stoner seemed unbeatable, on Friday he was two seconds quicker than everyone but Marco was fast too, fighting with him and Lorenzo. The great thing was that on Saturday, in qualifying, he snatched pole from him at the last second. It was a wonderful day for Marco, great payback: at your rival's home track, everyone's shouting at you, whistling at you and you take pole. This was one of those cases where you saw that the more difficulties there were, the stronger Marco would become.

The day of the race, seeing as the threat spoke of the starting line and alongside the track there is a fence with the public crowded behind, I said to the guys: 'Sorry but what about the race?' 'Not a problem.'

In fact there were many undercover agents, and then along the fence there was a row of uniformed police and no public. This was the most dramatic moment for me, with no public near the fence, this row of policemen, agents with binoculars watching the grandstands above the garages... If something were to happen they'd threatened that it would be at that moment.

Marco started badly, many said it was due to stress but I think he started badly just because it's something that sometimes happens. In that strange race he finished sixth.

ROSSELLA All of these things had an influence on his riding in the following races. He wasn't as relaxed as before; he had to pay special attention that nothing would happen.

SIMONCELLI DIDN'T CARE

PAOLO Marco completed fantastic practices at Silverstone too – it was him and Stoner battling once more. I remember that they were the only two to make the last turn right on the inside kerb, awesome! But Stoner took pole by a hair. Marco was second and naturally the day after there was rain for the race. Marco was very quick in the wet, but it wasn't damp there, there was water several centimetres deep on the track, loads of puddles. Stoner was in the lead, then Dovizioso, Marco right behind him, he'd passed him once but Andrea had got back ahead by crossing his line so Marco went a little slower to watch what he was doing and then pass him. The straight was a pool of water and as he passed Dovizioso, 20 centimetres from him, the bike got away from him and he did one of the longest slides anyone's ever seen and that's how it ended.

In Assen too he was very quick over the three days, no-one else got a look in. First, first, first, the only one to bother him a little in the final session was Spies. In qualifying he took pole and the day after it was raining, the track was partly damp. What tyres to use, not to use... he was so certain of winning that he didn't really engage his brain that time and at the third turn, the first left-hander, with tyres that were still cold, he crashed and took Lorenzo down with him, or rather he went sideways and was hit by Lorenzo who was behind him. Both of them rejoined and Lorenzo finished sixth, Marco ninth because it took him longer to get back on the bike. More controversy, open war against Simoncelli. The fact was that Simoncelli didn't care, we were continuing to move forward.

Moving on, we headed to Mugello – there were consumption issues there too. He finished fifth, he'd qualified third, a good race nonetheless but he didn't race as he'd hoped to. It wasn't what he expected but it went like that. There was a period during which Marco's bike wasn't fast anymore. Every Saturday he'd take risks to try and take pole, at one point he was riding on the limit just to make the second row. I believe (and some others also believe) that although they hadn't taken anything away, they weren't giving him anything new either, once they realised that Marco could bust Stoner's balls...

At Sachsenring he was sixth. At Laguna Seca he crashed again, but on the back of very solid practices. Marco had become a reality. Contact with Ducati started there and became increasingly concrete. Marco was a little sceptical at first but then, having spoken with Preziosi and with Claudio Domenicali, he continued to say: 'Well, these guys are really good.' He was really thinking about it, it was the start of negotiations for the year after, once his contract with Honda, which we were renewing for a third year, would have expired. I remember Preziosi's advice, he told him: 'Marco, I suggest you only sign for a year, because then you will come to us.'

After Laguna Seca we took one of our best ever holidays because there were three weeks before we would head to Brno and so our whole group, with Marco, his girlfriend, Martina, Rossella, Michele and Chiara, Carlo Pernat, Filippo Falsaperla, Paolo Scalera and his kids, we all spent a fortnight travelling around America. It was amazing, one of the best memories that we have in our lives are of those days in California with the guys.

PAOLO So anyway, one time he'd be fourth, the next time fifth, his races were always aggressive but it looked like Marco wasn't worthy of the podium. But then in Brno he went well in practice and started the race fifth. He didn't make a great start, and had Vale and Lorenzo ahead of him, but he made two great passes. In the end, to get past Lorenzo he made another lap so as not to bother him but then he made a pass that he still remembers now! Lorenzo had understood who Marco was. He'd understood it before everyone else.

And I think this was one of the few times that Marco settled – he could have closed second but he said: 'Today I'm not ruining anything, I'll be third.' So he kept Lorenzo behind him, Dovizioso in his sights... when he crossed the line I think it was one of the best moments of his career. In the photos I can see how extremely happy he is. From there, perhaps, he started to put all the controversy behind him.

As a result, in Indianapolis there was a contract renewal meeting between Nakamoto, Marco, me, Pernat and Suppo. I remember that that day I was really mad with Nakamoto, I told him that he'd treated Marco really badly in Brno and I added that Marco would have raced for them for free but after that behaviour they would have to pay Marco if they wanted him, or else he'd go to Ducati. In Brno Nakamoto had told him that he was 'lucky' to be on the podium, that he was third because someone had chosen the wrong tyre and crashed, but I think that he did it on purpose to keep the price low. I told him everything I was feeling as a father. In the end we sorted it all out with a meeting during the Grand Prix at Misano where we all met up again, but I could see that tension had been created and would only be resolved if Marco and Nakamoto spoke privately. At that point I asked the two of them to stay and talk alone and we all left. After ten minutes they came out smiling, hugging, happy. The deal was complete, Marco would ride for Honda again in 2012.

"SOMETIMES I WAS A LITTLE HARD WITH HIM, FOR EXAMPLE AT BRNO AFTER HIS FIRST PODIUM. HE GOT VERY ANGRY BUT I JUST WANTED TO MOTIVATE HIM BECAUSE I KNEW THAT HE COULD HAVE DONE BETTER. I THOUGHT WE WOULD BE CELEBRATING HIS FIRST WIN TOGETHER.,,

SHUHEI NAKAMOTO

It all started in Turkey, in a hotel bar. Marco and his dad approached me and asked me if I was available to manage him. Marco said it as if it was already a done deal, without me even answering yes or no! We spent two hours laughing together, normal people just wanting to have fun. Even though I intended to say yes straight away, I played a little hard to get, as you do. Ten days later we met up at a motorway service station in Cremona and I told him: 'Right, OK, I'm in'. A beautiful thing was born, because it started with his first contract with Gilera and then Marco won the world title…

I IMMEDIATELY GOT ON WELL WITH DAD AND MARCO, 'THE CAT AND THE FOX'.

Though he was more of a big brother than a dad. We would have fun, and became almost accomplices in creating havoc. Marco was congenial, he wanted to enjoy himself and have nice people around him, because frankly he didn't like moody people. As well as his spontaneity that you wouldn't find anywhere else, Marco created a group and was the leader of this group – he knew that those three, four people were the ones he could trust. There were always problems in the garage, but he was always the calmest of all, the most relaxed. Normally in racing it's the crew chief or manager calming the rider down right? No way! Even when things went badly it would be Marco to calm everyone down with his smile. It's a characteristic generally shared by those riders who don't consider racing a job and rather come to have fun, riders from another era.

When we had to renew the contract with Honda, we came to the final meeting after two months of stress and still no-one knew how it would go. There was me, Suppo, Gresini, Nakamoto, Nakamoto's deputy, the translator, Marco and his dad. Paolo's intuition led him to say: 'Let's leave them to talk alone'. He'd already spoken to Marco, he wasn't stupid! We were thrown out and the two of them stayed inside.

I SAID: 'IT'LL BE AT LEAST HALF AN HOUR.' THEY CAME OUT AFTER SEVEN MINUTES, I TIMED THEM, NAKAMOTO WAS LAUGHING LIKE A DRAIN!

He would laugh only with Marco, who would say stupid things to him... it was like something out of a comic strip!

Preparing Marco's contract meant going to his house: meetings took place with his dad, his mum, every so often Martina would come by... It was like making a family contract. This was his way of interpreting life.

A BATTLE TO JUSTIFY THE TICKET

PAOLO After Indianapolis we got to Misano, it was another of Marco's great races. I remember the comments in Monday's paper: 'A battle between Simoncelli, Spies and Dovizioso that justified buying a ticket', because up ahead of them nothing happened.

The race started, but Marco didn't! At a certain point, watching the screen, I said: 'But what was he thinking?' He started a moment after the others, but a moment there means losing five, six positions. So he started to grind, passing several riders, even Rossi in the end. For me it was a normal pass but others thought it was too aggressive. Marco was like that, if he had to pass, he'd pass. Then he went after Dovizioso, he passed him and, as usual, as soon as he was attacked by Marco it was as if Dovizioso's primal instincts would wake up and he'd pick up his pace, who knows why. Marco passed him, Dovizioso passed back, and in the meantime Spies reached them. On the final lap Dovizioso was in front, Marco behind him and Spies right on his heels. Through the turn after the straight Marco passed Dovizioso, Dovizioso crossed him, Marco held on around the outside, it was fantastic. Marco reached the straight first and they came to the Quercia. At the Quercia both Dovizioso and Spies passed him. I think Marco did great at that point because while those two were braking hard he realised that it was better to brake earlier and go up the inside. Sure enough, the two of them were braking hard, Marco up the inside managed to exit before them, they got to the downhill turn, Dovizioso tried again but Marco didn't let him pass and finished half a metre ahead of him. It was a fourth place, but a really fantastic race.

He passed Lorenzo at Aragon too, then he made a mistake through a turn, exited on the outside and finished fourth in the end, but he ran a great race. In my opinion he'd become the master of the MotoGP, the guy that everyone wanted to interview – his congeniality was spreading.

We got to Japan. The earthquake had happened in March, causing all the problems with the Fukushima plant and there was controversy in the World Championship too: 'Do we go? Do we not go?' Marco spoke out for himself, unlike other riders who said one thing in private and another in public for fear of being penalised. But he had really taken this thing to heart, because he didn't want to take risks, he wanted guarantees. The results of tests carried out by Dorna on Japanese soil came back and it looked like everything was OK. If the results say it's all OK you can't say: 'No, it's not true', but his friend Chiara is a doctor and through her he got hold of a Geiger counter to measure radiation. Before leaving for Japan we had gone up towards Piacenza to get it – I remember that we'd stopped just off the motorway and a load of cars and even some lorries stopped too, people that recognised him, we were blocking the traffic exiting the motorway at Piacenza.

NOTHING TO CHANCE

ROSSELLA On Chiara's advice Marco had got hold of preventative medicine, so that even if there was radiation his body would be able to fight it – he was fully kitted up. He really left nothing to chance, he was meticulous in his work.

THE 1000

PAOLO In the race Dovizioso messed up the start; he moved too early and caused Marco and Crutchlow, one behind the other on the grid, to follow suit. Marco got away well, rode a fantastic race and finished fourth. He would have been second had it not been for the ride through penalty for the false start. He had become so strong.

There at Motegi he finally got to test the 1000 that he'd be racing with the following year. He'd kept pushing Nakamoto to let him try it and there was controversy because the Japanese didn't want Aligi or other members of the team in the garage... In the end we decided that Aligi would stay, but outside like I did – we went to watch him on track. Marco was pleased with this 1000, but he couldn't make the most of the day and record a fast time because something broke. I'd never seen anything like it – he got to the garage, going downhill with the engine switched off and within three minutes the bike had disappeared onto the truck, heading back to Tokyo. Afterwards they had one of the longest debriefing sessions that Marco had ever taken part in, they really talked for the longest time. Marco gave them some suggestions and I remember that Kukubo, the designer, called him back to compliment him. The technicians were really enthusiastic having spoken with Marco, perhaps because he said something that they hadn't thought of. Marco was really pleased, and from there we went to Australia.

> **" I'VE NEVER KISSED THE BIKE, BUT WHEN SHE BEHAVES WELL I TELL HER: YOU'VE BEEN GOOD. "**

ON THE PODIUM

PAOLO I think that Phillip Island, along with Mugello, was one of Marco's favourite tracks, if not his absolute favourite. Once again he was immediately on the pace. Stoner was very strong there, but after Stoner there was Marco. In practice Marco crashed three times in the same place, on that slow downhill section, we joked about it afterwards. Then he rode an unbelievable race.

In the final laps it started to rain and he, like everyone else, had started on slicks. Dovizioso had got past him because Marco was second and trying not to take risks. Two laps from the end Dovizioso passed him. But Marco got back in front and finished ahead. I remember that when he saw me on the track he stopped and said: 'No, eh! I've been in front for the whole time and you want to screw me on the last lap?' He was really happy, having passed him at the start, then being passed before getting in front again – I think it was really satisfying for him. So he was on the podium, he threw his slider into the crowd. It was windy and wonderful with him with that hair – the photos of that podium show him in one of the happiest moments of his life.

It finished like that; he was really pleased and convinced himself at that point that in Malaysia he would win – because he'd done great in winter testing, because he felt so strong.

The next day we had a late flight, we were at Phillip Island and went to Rosa's restaurant, because he'd always go there to have breakfast. It was a beautiful day. Before getting in the car we went down to the jetty in the harbour. There were some fishermen that recognised him and asked him for some photos. He even had his photo taken with me, it's the one I put on my mobile. You only think about these things afterwards... But I remember that as we left he said: 'Anyway dad, we should never leave this place.'

6. MALAYSIA

S.I.C.

PAOLO Malaysia represented something very important and strange in Marco's life. I'd like to know more about Malaysia. During a religious convention I asked an Indian holy man and he told me that in recent years it's become the world's most spiritual place. I didn't know how to reply but for Marco it's the place that marked his life.

Firstly the track is called the Sepang International Circuit: Sic. The first time we went to Malaysia with the 125, Rossella and I arrived at the track and there were all these 'Sic' T-shirts in a shop there. Low down in one corner they'd written Sepang International Circuit but that 'Sic' was great. We looked at each other: 'What, are we already that famous?' and we plundered the place, we bought every shirt they had... that was Marco's first merchandising, albeit 'stolen'.

Marco won the 250 World Championship in Malaysia. It was in Malaysia that he had the accident in which he lost his memory and the one where he broke his scaphoid the first time. The first time he recorded the fastest MotoGP lap was in Malaysia, during testing in February 2011. He won the title without his helmet and he died without his helmet... When he died, I would ask Christ why this was the case.

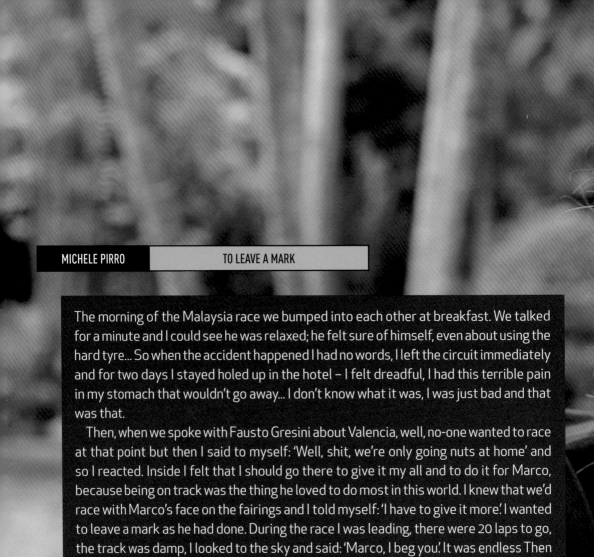

The morning of the Malaysia race we bumped into each other at breakfast. We talked for a minute and I could see he was relaxed; he felt sure of himself, even about using the hard tyre... So when the accident happened I had no words, I left the circuit immediately and for two days I stayed holed up in the hotel – I felt dreadful, I had this terrible pain in my stomach that wouldn't go away... I don't know what it was, I was just bad and that was that.

Then, when we spoke with Fausto Gresini about Valencia, well, no-one wanted to race at that point but then I said to myself: 'Well, shit, we're only going nuts at home' and so I reacted. Inside I felt that I should go there to give it my all and to do it for Marco, because being on track was the thing he loved to do most in this world. I knew that we'd race with Marco's face on the fairings and I told myself: 'I have to give it more'. I wanted to leave a mark as he had done. During the race I was leading, there were 20 laps to go, the track was damp, I looked to the sky and said: 'Marco, I beg you'. It was endless Then on the final lap I repeated: 'Come on Marco, don't mess with me, come on Marco, don't mess with me'. It was a release in the end. When I crossed the line I wanted to get out of there and maybe go into a garage, close it and not see anyone, be there alone. I took a very long time to get to parc fermé, like someone who didn't want to be there. Because the celebrating almost annoyed me.

SILENCE IN THE PADDOCK

PAOLO Marco had always suffered from respiratory problems and had even had an operation to straighten his nasal septum, so the humid heat of Malaysia was a problem for him. With 80 per cent humidity he was really unable to breathe, it was a huge physical effort for him.

And yet that first year in MotoGP he completed a great race in Malaysia – he was lying third until seven laps from the end but then he really couldn't take it anymore, he felt like he was going to faint and finished eighth. At the end of the race, despite finishing eighth, a Japanese engineer told him for the first time: 'Today the world has seen your potential.'

He prepared very thoroughly for the second year in MotoGP. He'd already started to follow a special diet the year before, he'd changed his mineral salts and he'd got an inflatable paddling pool, like those for kids, and he'd filled it up with ice... With 40-degree temperatures outside, you needed a pretty impressive physique and mental strength to throw yourself into that ice! I remember that the first time that he went in he wanted to get straight out, and I held him down as if trying to drown him, but after that initial shock he was fine and would go back in with no worries. This allowed him to lower his core temperature by a degree or two, so he was much better during the race. We'd also bought a vest that you'd put in the freezer and it would stay frozen: he'd put this on for 15 minutes before the race. After getting out of the pool, his teeth still chattering, he'd put the vest on as he was leaving the garage, removing it on the starting line.

On the starting grid we were all relaxed because he'd prepared well, maybe he needed another tenth or two, but he'd taken a couple from the box that his friend had given him, so he was really very well prepared. In these conditions, especially in Malaysia, Marco would put his wet towel – that we'd kept in the freezer – on his head to try and keep the heat out and stay cool even in those ten minutes on the grid. The only thing that I remember with regret about that race, the regret of my life, is that on the starting line I realised that he had that towel back to front. When I saw the reversed 58 I got chills, I instinctively wanted to get him to turn it around, but there were only five minutes to go and I told myself: 'I'm not going to distract him.' And that was that.

So anyway I helped him take his vest off, he did his leathers up, we hugged as usual and I took the scooter to watch the race trackside as I always did. The whole time he was in 250 I would always watch him on track, even in practice. But in MotoGP it's difficult for a parent to watch from the side of the track because it's scary... They have really tremendous bikes, the riders are animals and the bikes are animals. Actually, in my opinion, I think only four or five of them are able to really use these bikes to their full potential... Once the race began I immediately realised, right from the first turns, that he was having tyre trouble. Then on the second lap he passed in front of me and five seconds later he was dead. When I saw that helmet roll on the maxi-screen I really hoped it was someone else's, but inside I knew. I took the scooter, I went to the next turn, and when I got there the marshals were putting him on the stretcher. I helped them to load him into the ambulance and I knew that Marco had already gone. So I said goodbye to him, Marco's story finished there for me.

The scooter wouldn't restart, who knows why, I got to the clinic with a guy from Ducati who gave me a lift but I wasn't thinking: 'I hope he makes it', I knew full well that he was dead. At Sepang the rooms where the doctors work are behind glass, you could see everything, you could see their instruments and you could see everything they did. For half an hour they did things that I didn't even know you could do to a human body. There I thought: 'Shit, we're donating organs here' because egotistically I told myself: 'That way a part of Marco would live.' Instead the doctor told me that it wasn't possible because there'd been a cardiac arrest.

At that point I went into the room where they were trying to resuscitate him, I knelt down, took his right hand and continued to stroke it. The strange thing is that after the plane trip, when we reopened the coffin at home – because Marco was at home for 24 hours – that hand had remained soft. That was another of the things I can't explain.

When I left the clinic the thing that struck me was the silence in the paddock. That was usually a really chaotic moment, because the championship was on the move, so everything has to be loaded in a frenzied rush; there are forklifts loading the closed crates on to the trucks... But in those 300 metres to my garage there was a silence that stayed with me, total silence.

Aligi and Fausto stayed with me, we left together. I had a business class ticket and Malaysia Airlines were good enough to let us all travel in business, we joked about it because it was the first time that Aligi was travelling business class... It was Marco's parting gift, I'm sure of it. The rest is recent history and perhaps, up there, he is enjoying all of this attention.

THE DAY OF VICTORY

ROSSELLA The day of his 250 world title win was wonderful because naturally when Marco won we all went down underneath the podium but Paolo wasn't there. They did the prize-giving and Paolo was nowhere to be seen. Heck, we were worried and at one point I said to someone: 'Listen, take the scooter, go and see, because in this heat, with Marco winning etc I think he might have been taken ill.' We all looked around desperately and then Paolo was in the grandstand in front, on the other side of the starting line.

PAOLO The great thing was that I could see them and I knew they were looking for me. So I phoned Rossella, but she didn't answer. I also called Cuzari who was there but he didn't reply either and seeing as the grandstands are in front of the podium, and you have to go a long way round to get to the other side, I enjoyed watching the prize-giving from there. I was crying of course, because I was really moved. The people in the grandstands recognised me at one point – photos, slaps on the back... When I went down Rossella was coming to find me on foot and we crossed paths. It was wonderful.

AN 80-KILO DONKEY

PAOLO That title win was really a conquest for Marco, because the 250 story had begun in 2006 with some problems. In the World Championship there are some riders who, as good as they are, have got where they are because they are backed by a sponsor or because they're part of a project. Marco's rise on the other hand was solely down to personal merit.

The story had started like this – at that time the technicians there were Sandi and Brazzi, the 'good' guy and the 'bad' guy. I remember clearly that when Sacchi, the team manager, met us, he showed us a paper where it was written that Rossano Brazzi, former crew chief to Valentino Rossi, wanted Simoncelli for the following year. Marco was so excited, we put together a considerable contract and that was when we started to earn money, we were proud of that.

Everybody said that Brazzi was a difficult person, so much so that they called him 'Benito' Brazzi, but Marco would say: 'Well, I did three years with Matteoni, you'll see that it'll be fine with him too.' Instead we were faced with what was for us a new situation, a selfish team, verging on malicious.

We started with many positive words, like: 'This year we have time to learn.' But after only three World Championship races Brazzi went to Aprilia and said in a meeting: 'I can't do anything with an 80-kilo donkey.' His exact words, and uttered after only three races... This was Marco's environment!

After that meeting we went to Le Mans and, in my opinion, Marco rode a good race but along the straight with Barberá he realised that his bike was inferior, he'd pass him as and when he liked.

Having finished the race eighth Marco came back to the garage, a mechanic took the bike but no-one looked him in the eye, as if he didn't exist. And Brazzi said: 'Right, let's go and eat' and all the mechanics followed him. They left him there like a fucking idiot. So Marco came to me and said: 'Dad, the bike wouldn't go for shit today', and I told him, 'Right, when he comes back you go and tell him because these things need to be said here.' He forced himself to do it, when Brazzi returned he started to approach him: 'So, Rossano?' 'Well! If you think I'm going around the world with all these people, spending money to do races like that, then you haven't understood a thing! You two had better get moving!' He spoke loudly to make himself heard and was referring also to Corsi, who hadn't done well in that race.

At that point Marco said: 'Yes, OK, I need to get moving but the bike was really shit today!' Brazzi was like a boxer who'd taken a punch to the face, no-one had ever had the guts to answer back to him like that. Brazzi liked to stay within the set-up parameters that Valentino used. But Marco weighed 20 kilos more than Valentino! I clearly remember that 90 per cent of his problem was always the same: 'The bike goes wide as I exit, it goes wide, it goes wide.' And Brazzi would reply: 'Well, look, we're within the parameters. You, you have to pull.' He had to use his body to pull it, we couldn't go outside those parameters because they couldn't imagine a bike different to that which Valentino had won with. Instead all it needed was a stiffer spring at the rear, as Aligi used later.

> **"IN BIKE RACING, IN MY OPINION, THE RIDER COUNTS MORE, BUT YOU'RE NOT EXACTLY RUNNING ON FOOT, YOU'RE ON A BIKE, SO IF THE BIKE IS SHIT THEN YOU STRUGGLE TO WORK MAGIC. "**

TIMES OF CRISIS

ROSSELLA It was 2006, I was in Malaysia too, with Martina, Marco, Paolo and his sister Angela. We went to a restaurant to eat with the team because Marco always liked to do that. They arrived a minute before us, when we arrived they were already seated and there was no space so we sat at a table right next to them. These mechanics didn't even turn to say hello – they were joking amongst themselves, sharing photos, laughing, Marco tried to join in, he was facing them and tried to be part of the group. But he wasn't allowed; they acted as if we, right there next to them, didn't exist.

I didn't care about us, but I was sorry for Marco as he was their rider and part of the team! That year he suffered terribly, they really treated him badly. It was an awful year... a boy of that age, who's just changed category, you kill him like that. Marco had some times of crisis, luckily he came through them because in certain situations it only takes a second to go down the wrong path. He came out of it well, but no thanks to them.

IT SEIZED

PAOLO At Mugello Marco had a fantastic race – he led up until five laps from the end, but when it was time to fight for the finish, his piston seized at the end of the straight. He managed to keep from falling by pulling the clutch, he rejoined and finished seventh. When he got to the garage Brazzi asked him: 'What happened?' Marco: 'Um, I think the piston seized.' And Brazzi: 'After 20 laps it seizes?' And him: 'Well open the engine and you'll see.' Marco went away and came back after half an hour to find Brazzi with the piston in his hand: 'And so?' 'Um... it seized.'

Brazzi didn't come to Barcelona because he had quite a serious inner-ear infection which meant he couldn't even stand up. So we had a bewildered team as Brazzi, despite his character, was a technician and the boss. The others only knew how to use the tools and be mechanics, but no-one knew how to map the engine, they were there without the person who'd tell them what to do and even what to eat, with a young rider... So they gave us the engineer from the test team, a really good person who was also very good at his job, but with no track experience. In the test team you have all the time you want, while at a Grand Prix it's a bit different, you don't have time, you have to fit everything into an hour. Basically it got worse at each race, we always had problems. Marco began to crash often, because he'd always been a warrior, for better or worse, he wasn't one of those who'd say: 'Oh, the bike's not right so I'll go slower.'

With practice over, Marco shared his impressions with this engineer and he'd pick up the phone and call Brazzi who'd tell him what to do with the bike without even speaking to the rider... a total mess. Anyway, one way or another, we managed to finish the season in this unbelievable environment, with the team that would get to the garage in the morning and not even say hello anymore. The only person we had any kind of relationship with was Guido, the telemetrist, who stood apart from the crowd.

First I want to say that in Italian I would say I was Sic's 'preparatore atletico' and not his 'personal trainer', an Americanism that I don't like.

I started to work with Marco because he had the same physiotherapist at the Clinica Mobile as Vale, Marco Montanari, and he told me: 'Look, I have a guy who could do with coming to you.' 'OK, I'll talk about it with Vale,' I said. Vale said yes but it's not like I went to Marco and said: 'You have to work with me', that would have been presumptuous. We'd see each other at races, say hi, I was a fan of his because he was one of Vale's friends.

Then, in 2006, he came to speak to me and I got a bit paranoid there, thinking: 'But let's say that one day he becomes strong, I will find him competing against Vale, what the hell will I do?' But instead it was Vale who insisted, and it all worked out perfectly. Actually, he set me a challenge: 'Let's see how good you really are, it's easy to train Valentino Rossi...'

Marco's first year in 250 was 2006, he wasn't doing well and when he came to me we immediately realised that he wasn't exactly in tiptop shape to ride the bike. On his first day at the gym I explained everything to him: 'Look Marco, we alternate the days with the changing rooms here, male and female, because the sauna and Turkish bath are only on one side...' 'OK, OK,' he said. On the second day he arrived and asked: 'Oh, Carlo, where are the changing rooms today?' And I, as a joke, pointed to the ladies. He went in, got changed, came out, trained and then went back in to take a shower. When he came back out he was laughing like crazy and I couldn't understand why, I hadn't noticed which changing rooms he'd gone into! 'Marco what the hell did you do?' 'Nooo! You told me to use the changing rooms marked "women"... Obviously when he'd gone in to change there was no-one there, but when he got out of the shower he realised there were women in there, but he was already in his bathrobe. He started to say hi to them, 'Ciao, ciao' and they left, embarrassed, while he finished drying his hair before coming out. 'I was already there, what should I have done?' he said.

That was Marco's second day, to give you an idea...

Another great episode was... well, let's say that Marco was well endowed, he had a big dick. One day I was talking to him in my office when Michele Maggioli came in – he plays basketball in the A series and also trains with us – and said: 'Oh Carlo, there's a guy in the changing room with a massive cock! I play with a load of black guys, I've seen some dicks, but never one like this!'

And Marco, who was there with me, immediately entered into the competitive spirit: 'Let's go and see!' he went in there but the guy had already got dressed.

'We came to see...' Marco told him.

And the guy: 'No, well I'm dressed now...'

Bottom line – Marco came back, disappointed: 'It didn't go well, I didn't see it...'

WE CALLED HIM 'THE SALESMAN' BECAUSE OF THE DISTANCES HE'D DRIVE IN HIS CAR EACH DAY. 'HAVE YOU DONE 1,000KM TODAY?' I'D ASK HIM. 'IF NOT, YOU NEED TO GET OUT THERE AND DRIVE, EH?'

I knew when Marco arrived each day because I'd hear him skidding... in the car park outside there's a piece of linoleum, perfect for sliding. And every time he arrived, especially in the early afternoon when the car park was a little emptier, he'd make some impressive slides... for a minute, a minute and a half. It was an interrupted whistle of rubber, amazing. At the start Vale would do it too but then he stopped, let's say he'd grown up.

After he'd been coming to the gym for a while he got into another scrape. There's a big roundabout nearby, Marco skidded but as he exited he went wide, crashed and broke the steering column. 'What do I do? My dad will be mad,' he said when he got to the gym.

I told him: 'Look, take it to Marcello, he'll fix it for you straight away.' Marcello is the Rossi family's long-time trusted mechanic and when someone has a problem like that he's quick and good. So Marco took the car there and Marcello fixed it up in a couple of days. In the meantime he told his dad everything, and he went mad anyway. Marco went to pick the car up, came to the gym and at the same roundabout, at the same point, did the same thing again and broke the steering column again. So he went back to the mechanic but this time he was scared to tell Paolo the truth, so he said: 'Dad, Marcello didn't even fix the car properly, it looks like he doesn't understand anything...' And Paolo got pissed off with Marcello! They didn't tell him the truth until a couple of years later.

A NEW TEAM

PAOLO In 2006 we had a two-year contract with Aprilia, so we should have had one more year with the factory team and factory bike. Instead, before Christmas, engineer Dall'Igna and Sacchi asked us up to Noale to tell us that they wouldn't give Marco the factory bike. He was really upset and asked why, but they wouldn't give him an answer. I gave him the answer, in front of them, telling him that this was punishment because Marco had dared to criticise Brazzi.

They know they were not respecting the contract and they got around it like this – we'll take your factory bike away but we'll extend your contract by a year. I think we were smart to accept, and at that point they asked us to think about a new team.

Sometimes I think about life's strange turns. Aligi Deganello, who was in Fiorenzo Caponera's team when Marco was in 125, had had a motorcycle accident and the team had let him go. He had never been Marco's crew chief but we knew him well, and in 2005 we'd also been together in Rio as we'd gone to see Christ the Redeemer at Corcovado with both Aligi's and Marco's team. We lost each other along the way so when we got to Corcovado to take photos there was only me, Marco and Aligi – that photo was, I think, a premonition.

Two years later, when we asked him if he was available, Aligi didn't even think about it and said yes, then he put together an outstanding team, by raking here and there through the people that he and Marco knew. In the end Marco, with his way of doing things, was able to build a fantastic team that would follow him everywhere.

> " IN MY OPINION, ONE THING THAT HELPS YOU TO BE MORE COURAGEOUS IN LIFE IS HAVING AN OBJECTIVE. "

They introduced me to Marco at Jerez, it was the first Grand Prix of 2006, where he crashed out after just a few laps. We were on the steps to the clinic and someone said: 'This is Paolo, the physiotherapist, this is Marco Simoncelli.'

'Yes, yes, but I know him!' I instinctively said, because I would watch him on television.

Marco shook my hand: 'Pleased to meet you! But you know you looked better with a beard?'

'But I've never had a beard...'

And him: 'Well, grow one!'

Every so often, with the changes in climate and time zone, Marco would get a blocked intestine. He came to me once and said: 'I've got a problem – I haven't been to the bathroom in two days'. 'Look,' I told him, 'I'm an osteopath; I know some treatments that might work. Let's try and see, the worst that can happen is that it won't change anything.' And so that's what we did. The next morning he came in to the clinic – it was full of riders and journalists – and he shouted: 'Paolo!'

'Tell me!'

'You really did give me a shit massage!'

He had a bit of a problem with Bautista. Once, I don't remember what track we were at, we were watching a Superbike race on TV and saw a rider who was pulling a wheelie right on the finish line, certain that he'd won but then another guy came up out of nowhere and passed him, zip! Marco started laughing like mad: 'Come on, you can't do a stupid thing like that!'

'Shit, that was like something Fantozzi would do...' I said.

And him: 'More Bautista than Fantozzi!' Bautista was behind us getting a massage so I punched Marco in the side to let him know. But he, calm as anything: 'Oh, well it's not my fault... It's Bautista who messes up!'

When Marco started working with me he was a raw talent, both physically and in terms of his riding and here I think that Vale helped him a lot, in his approach to racing and when it came to certain lines... something that I don't get involved in because I could do huge damage. But Vale would give him good advice, it was cool. But me, Uccio and Albi, at the end of the race, would really give Marco a hard time, especially if he hadn't done well: 'You let yourself get fucked like a chicken!' and so on, just to wind him up. While Vale would say: 'But no, come on, well done, it's a podium...' He'd also try and defend him when it came to the Safety Commission because Lorenzo and the other riders, who work hard on using the media to psychological effect, had started to put pressure on Marco. They'd realised he was strong. The day before the famous Le Mans–Pedrosa incident Vale said to him: 'Marco tomorrow, during the race, I suggest... Well with everything that's happened let's try and not do anything stupid.'

And Marco: 'Yes, yes, don't worry, tomorrow... It's true, you're right!'

The next day was race day and Marco knocked Pedrosa off. When they saw each other back at the gym Vale said: 'Marco, what on earth...?'

'Well, I was there, I wanted to make a momentous pass...'

He wasn't trying to play dirty, he just wanted to make a pass that would go down in history. And in his own way he succeeded.

At the start, on a physical level, Marco was at zero, we laughed so hard. Doing leg extensions for example he would do four kilos! Four kilos!

I didn't want to believe it: 'Are you taking the piss?'

'No, no, no!' his leg was shaking, 'I can't do it!' He'd trained a lot before too, but I think he'd been doing it wrong.

In addition, he liked to eat a lot. If he were a normal kid it wouldn't have been a problem, because he had a great physique, but for a motorcycle rider... He'd easily get up to 85, 86 kilos and that was no good, especially in 250. When he won the 250 world title he weighed 75 kilos and his parents were worried because there was nothing of him.

Marco came to me every day and he'd train for between two and a half and four hours. At first he'd come in the late morning, then in the early afternoon, then in the evening. For a while he brought his grandma to the gym too – she'd broken her heel and had to do physiotherapy. But she was 84 years old; she'd exercise for three-quarters of an hour, an hour at most, while he'd train for three and a half hours! Once grandma had finished her routine she'd find a quiet corner and knit a jumper but Marco wouldn't leave her in peace.

'But no, what are you doing? Do the bicycle again!'

'No, Marco, leave her be, you'll kill her, poor woman!'

'But Marco, I'm tired,' she'd say.

'No, come on grandma! Shit, can't we find anything for her to do?'

'No, we can't! That's enough Marco!' I'd say. Then, after four hours at the gym he'd take her to Gresini's, to the racing department. They'd basically leave home at two in the afternoon and he'd take her home at ten at night.

Marco demanded so much from himself. Maybe at the start he wanted to make it, but he wasn't clear about what he had to do. He wanted to win but didn't know how. And when we met he was in a difficult situation due to his way of doing things, he'd tend to downplay everything, even when things weren't going so well... Behaving like that might make you appear more stupid than you are, but it was just a way to cover up what he was really feeling. I saw a lot of myself in him. He was precise in his way, I never once had to tell him: 'Marco, come and train today because you didn't come yesterday.'

I CONSIDER MYSELF FORTUNATE. I WOULD HOPE THAT I'M THE BEST IN THE WORLD AT WHAT I DO, BUT THERE'S PROBABLY SOMEONE BETTER THAN ME WHO JUST WASN'T LUCKY ENOUGH TO RUN INTO MARCO SIMONCELLI AND VALENTINO ROSSI.

Those who don't know the history behind Marco and Vale's friendship find it hard to understand how they were able to get on so well, despite the competition. But Vale really saw him as a younger brother, and Marco saw Vale as an older brother. I would hear comments from those around them, perhaps someone would try to make trouble but they always carried on and didn't give a shit. They'd ask about each other, they'd happily train together, then maybe they'd go riding at the Cava... It was great because we worked hard and had fun together.

MARCO WAS SPECIAL IN THIS WAY – HE'D ALWAYS MAKE YOU FEEL GOOD.

When he moved to MotoGP, his work load increased. I told him straight: 'In my opinion you deserve a trainer that can give you 100 per cent of his time, I can't, I've been with Vale for ten years ... I'm saying this out of respect for you...' But he chose to stay with us anyway.

HE HAD WON US ALL OVER, BECAUSE HE WAS AFFECTIONATE.

Once, it was the start of 2011, he had to go from Malaysia to Japan to test in the wind tunnel but Paolo didn't go with him: 'Lord, it's the first time I'm alone... at the airport alone, I almost wanted to cry!' When he told me I almost started to cry too!

A CARESS

ROSSELLA Marco got on well with his team because there was reciprocal love: he'd give and receive, give and receive, also because he was able to make everyone love him.

Marco was very physical, he'd want to touch you, feel you. When he was little he'd wreck my cheeks, the skin would be all inflamed! We'd be in the street perhaps, hand in hand, and he'd go: 'Mum, let me give you a caress!' I had to bend down and let him do it. To be honest, sometimes I wanted to say: 'Stop it Marco, I've had enough!' but I never did. When he stopped doing it I was almost sad. Later, all grown up, we might be on the sofa together and he'd put his feet on me and say: 'Mum, give me a massage!' and he'd laugh. He loved that.

A few years ago we had gone to Livigno, Kate wasn't there but she would come for the weekend so we had two rooms, one for us and one for them. The night Kate wasn't there we heard a knock on our door at one point – it was Marco: 'I don't want to sleep on my own in there, I'm coming to sleep here with you!' He'd do it when he was small too. In the summer, when we had the ice-cream parlour, he'd often sleep at my parents' because I'd leave him with them. In the morning he'd get out of bed and get into their big bed, in between them, and fall asleep again. In his sleep he'd start cuddling my mum or my dad then when he'd wake, opening his eyes and seeing that it wasn't me, he'd pull his hand back!

Other times, when I was heading out of the house and he was in his room, I'd shout goodbye: 'Ciao Marco, I'm off, OK?' Marco would run down the stairs.

'Yes! Ciao mum... MUM, WAIT, HANG ON!' Thump thump thump, 'Wait, a kiss!' he'd come down to give me a kiss. I loved it.

I also loved it when he was at the computer and maybe I was upstairs making the beds or cleaning and he'd go: 'Mum, come here... Listen, do you like this song?' He'd often call out to me. And in every case, from the silliest things to the most important, the last word had to be mine.

I remember an episode when he was racing in 250, it was 2007 or 2008. On the Sunday evening we were all in Berto's truck with his team, we were happy so it must have been a good race. We were all laughing and joking together. I was sat a bit further down the truck. Marco came over at one point, took my hand and held it for the longest time. It really had an effect on me, seeing

this 20-year-old guy come over to his mum, in front of all his mechanics, and hold her hand for 15 minutes! Normally kids think that the less the parents are around, the better... It was wonderful. And another time we were in Sydney – Marco and Paolo were heading to Japan the next day while Martina and Angela and I were going to stay there for ten days. That evening we had dinner together down by the harbour, we'd left the restaurant and were walking who knows where. Marco put his arm around me and we walked along like that – I loved it.

My biggest hope is that you make the most of your life and that you savour, with awareness, the good and the bad that it will bring.
The little things and the big things, without giving up in the face of difficulty, when you want to achieve a goal that you feel is right for you.

From Rossella's diary, 1995

Marco was the expression of happiness and it was an internal thing that actually grew inside him, beyond everything that life offered him. Perhaps he should have been angry, he could have been sad because it was that kind of moment, but essentially he was joyful, serene, always positive. And that was truly what I had hoped for in raising a son. I always said that my goal as a parent was to raise a child that is happy and aware. And with him I had succeeded 100 per cent.

I considered it a huge achievement that Marco, after all that he had done, had stayed the same. I remember that Sanchini, after Marco's world title win, made a wonderful box containing Marco's entire career up to that win. And I told him: 'Marco, it's touching. But the best thing is that you've stayed the same, identical.' Even Marco's friends were still those from school. And to the old friends he'd added many new ones. And then the old became friends with the new, because Marco would get everyone together, he was able to make one big family. Marco cared about so many people and was capable of caring about even more without ever taking anything away from anyone – he was very strong because he had all his love around him. If something had ever happened to him... if something had gone wrong with his girlfriend it would have been the end. Or if one of us had passed away, or if we had separated, it would have been really harmful to him, because his equilibrium was based on his emotions.

One day, he'd have been 12 or 13, he asked me: 'Mum, but if you died would dad be able to live?'

'I think so,' I replied.

'Why?'

'Because dad is strong – he'd suffer but he'd make it.'

'And you, if dad died?'

'I'd manage to live too.'

'I don't know if I'd be able to,' he told me.

It comes to mind that... he's solved that problem now.

FULL THROTTLE

PAOLO The second year in 250 started like that, with a standard bike but the right environment. Aligi is a wonderful person, Marco had found a personal guru in him, and had started to grow, to not do stupid things anymore, to stay calm. Psychologically he'd become stronger and was getting into incredible physical shape because he'd started to train with Carlo Casabianca, who's also Valentino Rossi's trainer. Marco was very happy and had started 2008 with an amazing mental charge – even though they hadn't given him the factory bike – because he'd worked hard over the winter. Aligi and I said: 'Let's not get carried away worrying, we'll work with what we have and we'll see.'

That year Bautista should have won, he was Aprilia's pick for the title but when we arrived in Jerez for winter testing we beat him... Marco was one of the fastest in every test and we were really hyped up when we got to the start of the championship.

The first race was in Qatar, at night. The practices went really well, even though he'd didn't take pole because in the last section of the track you need a lot of power. The track is divided into four sectors: Marco would get to T3 with a red helmet signalling the best time but then he'd lose three-, four-tenths through T4 because he weighed more and didn't have the engine that others had.

So he started second, and already at the start the bike would be switching off and then going again. He was twelfth, thirteenth, the bike switched off and he, ever faithful to his way of being, went full throttle to make up for it, ending up on the kerb before being thrown into the air. That was the only time during Marco's career that I saw him cry out of desperation – he'd shown he was strong, he was ready to collect and yet in the race he found himself with nothing, it was like a curse. They even interviewed him

while he was crying, and it was the only time I saw him throw his helmet on the ground, because Marco never did that kind of thing, in fact he refused to. When I went to get him he was really desperate, with everyone there consoling him, then it came out that it was down to an electronic error – the technician doing the mapping had forgotten to update Marco's.

Jerez was another great race. Marco started up front with Bautista and they stuck with each other through the race, passing each other time and again. On the final lap Marco was ahead, he let him past to keep him under control and through the long turn Bautista touched him. Everyone immediately picked on Marco, the Spaniards already had a problem with him but, strangely, when the two of them got up out of the dust, instead of coming to blows they hugged each other as if nothing had happened. And that Bautista is really a live wire. In the garage everyone blamed Marco, saying he was crazy but when Bautista arrived he said: 'The piston seized, the bike stopped, that's why he made contact.' Anyway, two races, two zeros. It was an uphill climb from there.

In Portugal Marco scored his first 250 podium. Then in Mugello he had another amazing race, with this bike that was a lot slower than the factory bikes in terms of top speed, but he pushed so hard that he reached the final lap together with Barberá. Marco passed him through the turn, Barberá got back in front on the straight. On the last lap Marco moved to the left on the straight but Barberá had decided to pass him at exactly that moment. In my opinion he wasn't looking forward but at the tank, so he touched Marco with the brake, it got him on the bum, Barberá's front wheel locked and he took flight. Fortunately he didn't hurt himself. Marco finished the race and won it – it was his first win in 250.

After the race there were tears, joy and the usual controversy from the Spaniards who were starting to get worried about this kid. I remember that they were talking about it on *Fuorigiri*, everyone said their piece and then they interviewed Barberá who said: 'He stretched his leg wide and took the brake.' This is proof that he wasn't looking ahead and wanted to pass as closely as possible just to scare him... Marco's reply on live television? 'Your sister stretches her legs wide!'

In Barcelona there is a really long straight, 1.3km, so the engine counts for a lot. Marco weighed more and found himself fighting with Bautista. During the first laps Marco passed him at the end of the straight, before the start line, and I think this conditioned the whole race. He threw himself in and took the lead on lap one and on lap two. The race developed, Bautista built a bit of a lead, but not much, five, ten metres. They reached the final lap and Marco tried everything to pass him but couldn't do it. They got to the slow, first-gear turn at the end of the straight and Bautista, remembering that Marco had passed him there, braked harder and went long. Marco passed him on the inside and snatched his second race win in a row right on the line.

At Donington there was another great battle between Marco with the private bike and Bautista with the real factory bike.

Marco had always gone well at Donington and that year it went to the wire. Together with Bautista there was also Kallio with the KTM, who'd tipped the balance in Aprilia's decision to give Marco the factory bike.

At the final turn Marco was behind Bautista: he braked hard and didn't touch him but went a bit wide, taking Bautista wide too. Kallio, who was third, went up the inside to take the lead. Marco's last lap was unbelievable, I think he did a lap record, but he couldn't take Kallio and finished second.

They came back to the garage, parc fermé, all angry, Martinez was railing against Marco as usual and Marco said: 'But I'm not Bautista's wingman. What the hell does he want from me?' I liked that.

Anyway, Bautista wasn't able to win and so for Aprilia there were two things that weren't going well: the first, KTM was leading the World Championship; the second, that Marco was winning races with a standard bike. Aprilia's engineers had spent a great deal of money on the RSA and yet this crazy kid, riding an LE that should been losing out at every track, was able to bother them. As a result a TV and press campaign was triggered, telling Aprilia to give Marco the factory bike and in the end the factory bike arrived. We went to Brno to test it and Marco, after only two laps, realised that it was another thing entirely. Many people, even friends like Pasini, discouraged him because it would break: 'Don't take it, you're fast with the LE. This one has a load of defects...' they told him.

And in Sachsenring with the factory bike he took pole and then won the race in style, and in the wet no less. He trounced them... Was this the bike that wouldn't go?

At Indianapolis the race was cancelled due to bad weather but Marco had taken pole, then in Japan he made another of what I consider to be his best races. He'd gone great in practice. Marco immediately took the lead in the race, Bautista made a good recovery and after 15 laps he reached him. At that point Bautista must have thought: 'It's done.' So he shilly-shallied behind Marco for a bit and then when he decided to pass him he realised it wasn't that easy.

On his first attempt Marco closed the door, Bautista almost crashed. Marco started to lap faster and faster, he wasn't at the limit, he still had something more. The last lap was fantastic, with Marco building an advantage of five- or six-tenths and holding it to the end. Bautista had been well and truly beaten and Marco was out of his mind, he was ecstatic when he got to parc fermé. I remember that on that occasion Bautista went to engineer Dall'Igna and said these exact words: 'Gigi, but Marco's bike goes like mine, I can't pass him on the straight!' He went to complain because with this bike he couldn't pass him like he'd done with the LE!

Everybody advised us to continue the championship with the LE because they said that the RSA was fast but extremely difficult to set up. For many Marco was winning because he had the LE, but when we asked them to swap, everyone answered: 'No, but you've got to grips with this bike now.'

We got to Sachsenring with this RSA. As a first race we only had the one bike and so if Marco had a problem the spare bike would be totally different. We took this risk because we believed it was worth it, we had everyone's eyes on us, people who sneered: 'Now he'll stop winning, you'll see, now he'll pass him.' But he took pole and then it rained for the race while we'd only had four practice sessions in the dry.

For the setting we'd followed the indications we used with the LE, making the normal changes for the wet, softening the suspension, shortening the gear ratios. On the day of the race Marco came, saw and conquered... We were as happy as Larry while everyone else kept quiet.

With the race bike each gear has seven or eight possible options, so there are seven or eight firsts, seven or eight seconds etc. You, partly with the help of the data acquisition and partly from what the rider tells you, choose the gears. The engine of a 250 two-stroke twin has maximum power of about 13,200 revs so you need to do the gears so that you have maximum power at the right moment.

We call these maps telemetry although it would be more correct to call them track layouts. At the end of each session the electronics guy takes the fastest lap, or a lap that the rider highlights, and analyses each corner with the help of the bike's data acquisition, which has different sensors to read different parameters: the height of the suspension, top speed, the speed of each wheel... If you see there is a difference, for example if the back wheel is faster than the front wheel, it means that either he is sliding or the front wheel is wheelieing. Then, to understand if it's wheelieing or spinning you look at the positioning of the fork – if it's extended and the wheel is slower it means it's wheelieing, if the fork is low but the front wheel is slower it means it's spinning at the rear.

Based on this information you correct or confirm the gears, the suspension settings... You also take note of what the rider says. If he says: 'The bike goes wide', you need to fix it so that the front is a little lower and the rear a little higher, so you use slightly stiffer springs.

To win the race you need to make your best laps particularly towards the end, but that's not easy because by the end the tyres are worn, the rider is more tired, the engine gives less... The only advantage is that you have less fuel, everything else is worse.

During free practice we'd test the track, the temperature, the rider and we'd sort the setting, then in qualifying we'd use the first 25 minutes to further refine the bike and the last 20 to try and set a fast time.

To monitor and analyse the bike's reactions in different conditions and after making changes you fill in the technical data sheet. At the top, as well as practical information (the bike frame, circuit, date etc) there are the values and parameters of the bike and the environmental conditions, like the air and track temperature, humidity, time of day etc.

Each time the bike comes back to the garage and various adjustments and changes are made, this is noted on the sheet. In 250 free practice was at 11am and then you'd make changes before the afternoon session. Normally with the two-stroke engine (that no longer exists in the World Championship) new pistons are put in overnight so that when you start Saturday morning's practice you have a richer fuel mixture to avoid seizing and for quick bedding in, so for the second exit we make the mixture a little thinner, and we work on the setting and on strategy. We always make a note when fuel is taken out or added to decide how much fuel to carry for the race. Normally we'd start with 20 litres and wouldn't change, that way the rider would get used to it and would lap in practice with the bike that would get gradually lighter. Then you make changes for qualifying, and at the end of qualifying you put on a softer tyre to try and record a fast time.

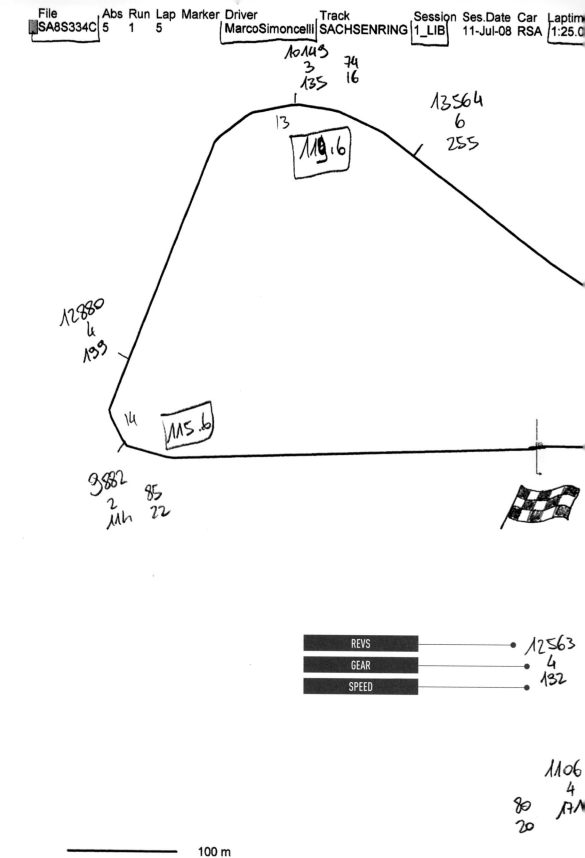

10143
3
135

74
16

13

119.6

13564
6
255

12880
4
199

14

115.6

9882
2
114

85
22

	REVS	12563
	GEAR	4
	SPEED	132

1106
4
80
20

171

100 m

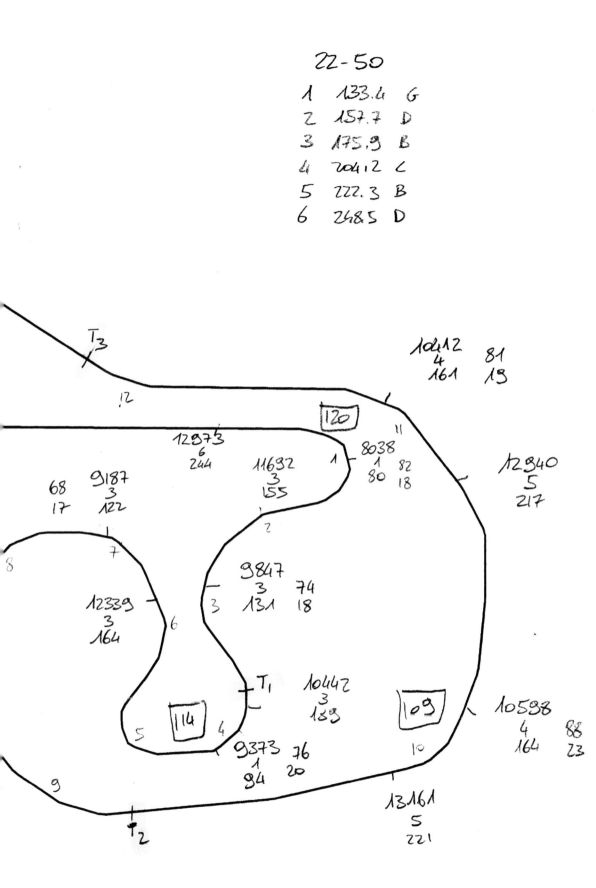

SQUADRA CORSE METIS GILERA

Circuito	SACHSENRING	L. 3.671	Pilota	SIMONCELLI # 58	Moto TCO 708 Sic 1	Data 11 – 07 – 2008

Telaio	Boccole ↑ – 7.5 ↓ – 4.5 – Off set 27.5 – Sfil. 13 mm.	Forcellone	F13 AP 709	L. 577.5	Pivot – 3

Forcella	TTX 08 – TXF 26 – Molle Ds. 7.0 (DF61 - L. 260) Sx. 7.1 (05F135 – 260) PL. 7 – C. 11 – R. 9 – Oil 170

Ammort.	AP25024 – R 132 – h. 342.5 – molla 84.1 (00R9 - L.150.1) pl. 10.5 – C. 9 – R. 22	Biellismo AP 702

Motore 2506 - 06	Cilindri APF ↑ 99 + 16 ↓ 4005 +16	Pistoni SP2103 08	Spinotti bomb. Km. 0	Teste AC 38 Gap 0,74
	Alberi motore ↑ 08 / 26 ↓ 08 / 25	km. 752	Bielle ↑ ↓	km. 752
	Tubi 102C ↑ N 128 ↓ N 127	km. 0	Collett. Sc. ↑ 36 ↓ 36	Silenz. D1 R. Km. 167
	↑ GP 267 – AK 874 3^ – G 236 – g 48 – aria 1.75 ↓ GP 267 – AK 872 3^ – G 232 – g 48 – aria 1.75 – V. 40

Accens.	Offset	+1	+1	+1	+0.5	+0.5	0	Pwm%	0	0	+5	+5	+10	+15
		+1	+1	+1	+0.5	+0.5	0		0	0	+5	+5	+10	+15

Curva N063A - B003V - B083W - B002X	Gomme: Ant. 05 286	Post. 3511	Mix 20 – 18 lt.

Cambio	1^ 14 - 30	2^ 16 - 29	3^ 16 - 26	4^ 15 - 21	5^ 14 - 18	6^ 20 - 23	Finali 22 - 50

Ox. 20,6 – 20,5 Tem. 25°/Gr.33° – 29°/Gr.41° Umidità 42 % – 38 % Pressione 972 – 971 Ora 11.15 – 15.10

Note:

	START	File	Nastro √	Modifiche
1				
2	1.31.61	111B.		
3	29.17	332 C		
4	28.15			
5	27.13			
6	BOX		↑ AK873 III – G 234 ↓ AK871 - G 228 // PWM ↑↓ I-VI - 5% - 10% // Nastro C // Amm Pl. 11.5
7	/	334C	Post. 3483
8	25.73		
9	25.70		
10	25.07		
11	25.00		
12	25.47	T4	
13	Box		↓ PWM Tutto – 5% // Strategia 1.000 - 1.450 PWM. - 5% // Ant. 04286
14	/	335C	Amm. 31 molla ff.1 Pl. 10.5 // R. 20
15	26.57		
16	26.20		
17	BOX		Off-set. 25 // Fork Pl. 8
18	/	336..	√√
19	25.17	T3	
20	26.50		
21	25.16		
22	BOX		Tolt: fbt. // Finali 21-48 - Forcell. 574.4 // Interax: 2 // Fork C.10 - 0.8 150 mm. // Offset
23	START	QUAL.	I-II-III +0.5° IV-V - 0.5° // Ant. 6680 Post. 6167
24	27.27	337	
25	26.54		
26	26.10		
27	BOX		PWM ↑ tutto - 10% ↓ tutto - 15% // Fork Pl. 9 // Post. 3483
28	/	338C	
29	25.21		
30	24.90		
31	24.97		
32	24.62		
33	24.70		
34	25.36		
35	BOX		Strategia 1.300 - 1.450 Adv - 0.5° // ↑ G 232 ↓ 225 // Ant. 04286 Post. 3483
36		335C	Amm. Pl. 10,25 – R 18
37	24.66	T2-T3	
38	24.53	T3	
39	24.27	T1-T2-T3	
40	24.65	T1	
41	BOX		Post. 3483
42	/	340C	
43	37.46		
44	23.95	T1-T2-T3	Lib. 81 Km. Qual. 84 km.
45	BOX		Tot. 165 km. Tolt: 6 lt.

SQUADRA CORSE METIS GILERA

Circuito	SACHSENRING	L. 3.671	Pilota SIMONCELLI # 58	Moto TCO 708 Sic **1**	Data 13 – 07 – 2008

Telaio	Boccole ↑ – 7.5 ↓ – 4.5 – Off set 25 – Sfil. 14 mm.	Forcellone	F13 AP 709	L. 574.5	Pivot – 4

Forcella TTX 08 – TXF 26 – Molle Ds. 6.9 (04F126 - L. 260) Sx. 7.1 (05F135 – 260) PL. 6 – C. 13 – R. 10 – Oil 150

Ammort. AP25031 – R 132 – h. 342.5 – molla 80.6 (99A42 - L.148.6) pl. 10.5 – C. 9 – R. 25 | Biellismo AP 801

Motore 2506 - 26
- Cilindri APF ↑ 98 + 14 ↓ 4018 +16 | Pistoni SP2103 08 | Spinotti bomb. Km. 198 | Teste AC 38 Gap 0,74
- Alberi motore ↑ 08 / 45 ↓ 08 / 46 km. 198 | Bielle ↑ CtAa 21 ↓ CtAa 22 km. 198
- Tubi 102C ↑ N 128 ↓ N 127 km. 363 | Collett. Sc. ↑ 36 ↓ 36 | Silenz. R 1 Km. 198
- ↑ GP 267 – AK 875 3^ – G 238 – g 48 – aria 2 ↓ GP 267 – AK 872 3^ – G 232 – g 48 – aria 1.75 – V. 40

Accens. | Offset

						Pwm%	+5	+5	+5	+5	+5	+5
0	0	0	0	0	0		+5	+5	+5	+5	+5	+5
0	0	0	0	0	0							

Curva N063A - B003V - B083W – B002X | Gomme: Ant. 414 | Post. 465 | Mix 18 – 18 lt.

Cambio	1^ 14 – 30	2^ 16 – 29	3^ 16 – 26	4^ 15 – 21	5^ 14 – 18	6^ 20 – 23	Finali 21 – 49

Ox. 20.8 – 20.8 | Tem. 205° / RAIN – 24° / WET | Umidità 60 % – 66 % | Pressione 972 – 971 | Ora 9.10 – 12.15

Note: Catena, Pipette, Candele, Frizione km. 0 //

1	START	File	Nastro RAIN	Modifiche
2	1.42.93	W.UP		
3	40.14			
4	38.04			
5	36.84			
6	36.26			
7	35.77			
8	36.41			
9	34.98			
10	35.79			
11	35.17			
12	35.02			
13	BOX		Tolt: 11.2 Lt. / ↑ AK 874 III – G 236 ↓ G 230 // Ant. 414 Post. 465
14	ENTRATA			
15	RICOGNIZIONE			
16	START			
17	35.12			
18	34.45			
19	34.49			
20	33.94			
21	33.92			
22	33.85			
23	34.12			
24	34.37			
25	33.79			
26	34.48			
27	34.08			
28	34.07			
29	33.86			
30	34.01			
31	33.88			
32	33.74			
33	34.45			
34	34.22			
35	34.03			
36	35.67			
37	34.21			
38	34.36			
39	35.18			
40	34.65			
41	34.02		0	
42	34.06			
43	33.53		1	
44	34.1			
45	BOX		Tolti: 2 Lt. W.UP 48 Km. Gara 117 Km. Tot. 165 Km.

" TO BE STRONG AND TO BE WINNERS YOU NEED TO
BEAT THE CHEQUERED FLAG. "

WINNING THE WORLD TITLE

PAOLO Then we went to Australia, we won there too and then arrived in Malaysia. Winning the world title seemed simple, at least on paper, but then you need to actually do it, so it was a really challenging weekend. Marco's mum, his girlfriend, Martina, they were all there with us, only Aldo Drudi was missing. Even Marco would hold it against him: 'Damn, you should have been there!'

Malaysia, with the humidity, was Marco's weak point due to his respiratory problems. In Malaysia Aoyama and Bautista had always been fast but he started his practice sessions with no worries and the race began with four guys there at the front – Marco, Aoyama, Bautista and Simon. Marco needed to finish third to take the title but when Bautista started to bug him Marco couldn't ignore it. Bautista was leading and, in order to pass him, Marco almost had a highside through the fast turn after the S, I don't know how he managed to stay upright, but this proved that when something's meant to be it's meant to be. He was able to hold on but at that point he realised that it was probably better to settle, also because Simon had broken down in the meantime, so he could finish behind Bautista and Aoyama no problem.

I was in the grandstand, in the crowd, as I usually was and I saw that the last laps were really difficult – he'd slowed down, maybe when he decided to give up the fight his adrenalin had dropped, and he was dead tired... I could see that Takahashi was getting closer lap after lap and I was worried, because from where I was sat I couldn't tell how many laps were left. He managed to finish with a big wheelie, then he stopped on the pit-wall and put the commemorative T-shirt on that Drudi had prepared. He was back to front, the person that helped him put it on was not thinking straight, and he had it on backwards. But it was almost better like that.

HHHHH

ROSSELLA When he got to the wall, having crossed the line, he kept saying 'Hhhhh', he was thirsty! In the hump of the leathers riders have a flask with a straw coming out of it to quench their thirst but in that race something had happened, I think the straw had come unattached, meaning he couldn't drink. So afterwards he was totally dehydrated. 'Water, water!' he said, and when they gave him a bottle he threw it over his helmet, that's how hot he was!

To win the title Marco needed to finish that race third, but he wasn't used to settling. It was totally out of character to have to think: 'OK, here I should hold still, and not go and take second.' It was unnatural for him because that was not in his DNA. In the final laps he started to get edgy because the heat was making him bad. Marco had never coped well with Malaysia's temperatures, the humid heat really affected him, because he suffered from chronic rhinitis and so the temperature there was really the worst for him, he wasn't able to breathe. Those final laps were really very challenging. In fact afterwards, at the press conference, he said two words and then: 'Sorry, I can't do anymore!'

'What a title you've won Callaghan.'

This phrase refers to a joke that I'd told Marco and that had stuck in his head, and so this is why the mechanics did that board for him when he won the world title.

Callaghan is a well-to-do guy who gets up in the morning, opens his wardrobe and there are 30, 40 jackets and he says to himself: 'What jackets you have Callaghan!' Then he goes to his shoe cupboard, there's a row of shoes and he says again: 'What shoes you have Callaghan!' And so on with other things: socks, coats, shirts...

One day he goes to see his sister who's a cloistered nun. He gets to the convent, knocks and introduces himself: 'I'm Callaghan, I've come to see my sister.'

'But your sister's a nun, she can't see anyone, absolutely not!'

'But I'm her brother, Callaghan!'

'It doesn't matter who you are, this is a convent and your sister has married God.'

So he reluctantly leaves but then he thinks about it and says: 'Oh! What a brother-in-law you have Callaghan!'

'What a title you've won, Callaghan'

THEY'RE KIDS

PAOLO When Marco got to the finish line they were all at the pit-wall with a board prepared in secret by Eugenio the mechanic. 'What a title you've won Callaghan', which referred to a joke that Marco would always tell and that made him laugh so much, especially when Maurizio Pasini would tell it, it was deadly. It was a surprise, a nice thing, and in the evening we went to celebrate the title win.

Giampiero Sacchi took us to Modesto's, one of the most famous Italian restaurants in Kuala Lumpur. It starts with a quiet dinner, the guys from Mediaset TV were there too, Paolo, Meda, Porta, Magini, Cuzari also. Everything started out calmly and then at a certain point Guido Meda went over to Marco with a jug of water and threw it over his head. The fuse had been lit.

Apart from the 20 centimetres of water on the floor and the wall stained with wine, there's a wonderful scene that I'll always remember. All the guys were there, the mechanics and then Aligi and Giampiero Sacchi, the crew chief and sporting director, who should have adopted a certain level of behaviour. Giampiero went to Aligi who was sitting at the table and Aligi said to him: 'But Giampiero, look what a mess these guys have made here, cakes in faces, water, wine...' Giampiero, all serious, replied: 'Aligi, what can you do, they're kids!' and seeing as he was standing up next to him he poured a jug of sangria over his head... Hoorah, there was the real celebration!

In that moment the boss's cool head surprised me. After, as we left, I understand why they were relaxed... I don't know what the evening cost Giampiero but I'm certain that he covered part of it himself because if he'd put that bill in as part of the expenses I think Aprilia would have fired him! And I'll always remember that phrase: 'Aligi, what can you do, they're kids!' Fantastic.

CREDITS

> " I DON'T FEEL LIKE A HERO. I AM JUST LUCKY THAT MY PASSION, TO HAVE FUN AND GO FAST ON MY BIKE, HAS ALSO BECOME MY JOB. "

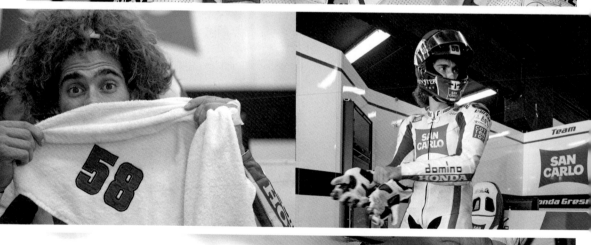

SIC

I was born in Cattolica on 20 January 1987. My parents had an ice-cream parlour and my dad loved bikes and racing. So I spent my childhood surrounded by ice-cream and engines! When I was four, my parents bought me my first bike, a Suzuki 50 minicross, for Christmas. And that's how I started bombing around the fields around my house. I started going minibike riding when I was about seven, and at nine I took part in my first official race in the regional championship.

Until I was thirteen I raced minibikes built by Mattia Pasini's dad, winning two Italian championships, in 1999 and 2000.

In 2000 I also tried a 125 Grand Prix bike for the first time and the following year I took part in the Honda Trophy and the 125GP championship with Massimo Matteoni's team, on a Honda. The first half of the season saw lots of crashes, the second half brought great results. I finished in ninth position in both the Honda Trophy and the Italian championship.

In 2002, aged 15, I took part in the European 125 championship, again with the Matteoni team but this time with an Aprilia. I won the championship and also debuted in the World Championship (at the Czech Grand Prix), taking the place of Jaroslav Hules in the last five races.

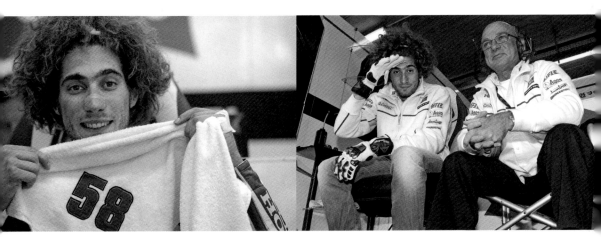

In 2003 I completed my first full World Championship season, still with team Matteoni and the 125 Aprilia. I finished the season in 21st position and my best result was fourth in the final Grand Prix of the year.

In 2004 I changed team, moving to Fiorenzo Caponera's outfit, and it was that year that I scored my first pole position, winning my first World Championship race. We were at Jerez, in the pouring rain and for the first time the Italian national anthem was played for me. There were various highs and lows that year and I missed the last two races through injury. I finished in eleventh place in the standings.

2005 was my final year in 125, and also the best. That year I won a race, reached the podium six times and finished the season fifth overall.

In 2006 I moved up to 250 with the Metis Gilera team and with a factory bike. It was a difficult season, full of miscommunication with the team and my crew chief. I finished the season tenth. My best race result was sixth.

For that reason Gilera took my factory bike away in 2007 and I was given an LE (a bike from 2005). The results didn't change much from the previous year but overall the season was a more positive one. Firstly I started working with Aligi Deganello and some of the guys that, still now, after five years, are a part of my team; today I have a great relationship with them. The other good thing was that we finally realised that we had potential.

In 2008 Gilera gave me an LE once again (but a bit more updated this time) instead of the factory RSA. The season got off to a shit start, with two zeros in the first two races but in the Portuguese Grand Prix I scored my first pole and my first podium and then, at my home GP of Mugello, my first 250 race win. Mid-season, seeing as I was leading the championship, Gilera finally gave me a factory RSA and from there things went really well. In total I scored seven poles, six wins, twelve podiums and the championship title with one round still to run.

The following year I decided to stay in the intermediate category and repeat my 2008 performance. The premise was there but one week before the start of the championship I broke my scaphoid while training on the MX bike. Not only could I not take part in the opening race, but the season turned into a disaster; each time that I thought I was back in the running, I would either crash or some technical problem would stop me from finishing the race. Despite all this I found myself fighting for the *title at the final race... Valencia. To win I needed to finish first and Hiroshi Aoyama thirteenth. We needed a miracle but there was still a chance.*

In the end he finished seventh and I crashed while leading the race. Game over! I finished third in the classification in the end, despite six wins and ten podiums.

Ah... In 2009 I also took part in the Imola round of the World Superbikes, standing in for Nakano on the Aprilia Superbike. It was a great day, which ended with a crash in race one and a podium in race two. That day the fans up on the hills around the track were really cheering me on... I still remember it today, it was fantastic!!! 2010 was the year of the big leap to MotoGP. After many years with the Piaggio Group I moved to Honda with Fausto Gresini's team. It was a very challenging and difficult year, because the level in MotoGP is so high. In addition me and my team (that came with me from 250) didn't have experience at the start and that made things more complicated. But by staying united and always giving it our all, we were able to make continuous improvement during the second half of the season, coming close to the frontrunners. In the end I finished eighth overall, having scored a best result of fourth (just missing out on third at the finish line).

2011 is a very positive year so far, because I am consistently as fast as the frontrunners, sometimes even faster! But unfortunately I still haven't managed to turn this speed into a podium.

Don't worry... I will continue to give it my all!!!

PS Rereading this I realised that I have 'a complicated relationship' with tenses... But I didn't want to write it all again! Make do with it! :)

Profile written by Marco for his Facebook page, 2011

RESULTS

1993
TRIED A MINIBIKE FOR
THE FIRST TIME

1999
ITALIAN MINIBIKE
CHAMPION

2000
ITALIAN MINIBIKE
CHAMPION

2001
MOVES TO 125

2008
MUGELLO, ITALY,
250 WORLD
CHAMPIONSHIP

2008
LE MANS, FRANCE,
250 WORLD
CHAMPIONSHIP

2008
ESTORIL, PORTUGAL,
250 WORLD
CHAMPIONSHIP

2006
MOVES TO 250

2008
BARCELONA, SPAIN,
250 WORLD
CHAMPIONSHIP

2008
DONINGTON,
UK, 250 WORLD
CHAMPIONSHIP

2008
ASSEN, THE
NETHERLANDS,
250 WORLD
CHAMPIONSHIP

2008
SACHSENRING, GERMANY,
250 WORLD CHAMPIONSHIP

2009
BRNO, CZECH REPUBLIC,
250 WORLD CHAMPIONSHIP

2009
SACHSENRING, GERMANY,
250 WORLD CHAMPIONSHIP

2009
ASSEN, THE
NETHERLANDS,
250 WORLD
CHAMPIONSHIP

2009
MUGELLO, ITALY,
250 WORLD
CHAMPIONSHIP

2009
INDIANAPOLIS, USA,
250 WORLD CHAMPIONSHIP

2011
PHILLIP ISLAND,
AUSTRALIA, MOTOGP
WORLD CHAMPIONSHIP

2002
EUROPEAN 125
CHAMPION

2004
JEREZ, SPAIN,
125 WORLD
CHAMPIONSHIP

2005
JEREZ, SPAIN,
125 WORLD
CHAMPIONSHIP

2005
BARCELONA,
SPAIN, 125 WORLD
CHAMPIONSHIP

2005
PHILLIP ISLAND, AUSTRALIA,
125 WORLD CHAMPIONSHIP

2005
LOSAIL, QATAR,
125 WORLD
CHAMPIONSHIP

2005
BRNO, CZECH REPUBLIC,
125 WORLD CHAMPIONSHIP

2005
SACHSENRING, GERMANY,
125 WORLD CHAMPIONSHIP

2008
BRNO, CZECH REPUBLIC,
250 WORLD CHAMPIONSHIP

2008
MOTEGI, JAPAN,
250 WORLD
CHAMPIONSHIP

2008
PHILLIP ISLAND, AUSTRALIA,
250 WORLD CHAMPIONSHIP

2008
SEPANG, MALAYSIA,
250 WORLD
CHAMPIONSHIP

2009
LE MANS, FRANCE,
250 WORLD
CHAMPIONSHIP

2009
JEREZ, SPAIN,
250 WORLD
CHAMPIONSHIP

2008
250 WORLD
CHAMPION

2008
VALENCIA, SPAIN,
250 WORLD CHAMPIONSHIP

2009
ESTORIL, PORTUGAL,
250 WORLD
CHAMPIONSHIP

2009
PHILLIP ISLAND, AUSTRALIA,
250 WORLD CHAMPIONSHIP

2009
SEPANG, MALAYSIA,
250 WORLD
CHAMPIONSHIP

2011
BRNO, CZECH REPUBLIC,
MOTOGP WORLD
CHAMPIONSHIP

2010
MOVES TO MOTOGP

FONDAZIONE ONLUS
Marco Simoncelli 58

The Fondazione Marco Simoncelli **was created with a view to helping those in need by supporting humanitarian projects and collaborating actively with public and private bodies and institutions in memory of Sic. The Foundation is a concrete symbol of the moral values that Marco demonstrated in such a genuine and sincere way.**

The Foundation's goal is to promote sport's commitment in support of social issues in order to contribute actively to the creation of humanitarian projects.

Through its charitable activities, the rider's family hopes to express its solidarity in support of the disadvantaged, particularly children and young people, as Marco already did for himself.

Thanks to its synergy with some of the longest-standing non-profit organisations, which have been working on issues of humanitarian solidarity for decades, and the precious support of so many of Marco's friends and fans, the Fondazione Marco Simoncelli works to support national and international projects.

Via Emilia, 9 – 47838 Riccione (RN) Italy
Tax code and VAT code: 03980340404
Phone: +39 3287653648
Secretary: info@marcosimoncellifondazione.it
Press Office: press@marcosimoncellifondazione.it

www.marcosimoncellifondazione.it

" I'D LIKE TO BE REMEMBERED AS
SOMEONE WHO KNEW HOW TO
THRILL WITH HIS RACING. "